The Girls Ate Last

Supriya Singh

Angsana Publications

First published in 2013

Angsana Publications
1 Banoon Road, Eltham, Vic 3095, Australia

National Library of Australia
Cataloguing-in-Publication entry:
    Singh, Supriya (Supriya S.) 1944 – The Girls Ate Last
    ISBN: 9780987569202 (paperback)
    Subjects: Kaur, Inder.
    Women – India – Biography.
    Women – Education – India
    Women – Social conditions – 20th century.
    Dewey Number: 370.82

Copy edited by Annette Ryan
Book design by Paul Ryan
Cover design by Christine Green
Photograph of the family 'bagh' on the cover by Janak Mistry
Author photograph by Katharine Dettmann

Also by the author:

On the Sulu Sea

Bank Negara Malaysia: The First 25 Years, 1959–1984

The Bankers: Australia's Leading Bankers Talk about Banking Today

Marriage Money: The Social Shaping of Money in Marriage and Banking

With love for Ranjan Bhaini

Contents

Map

Chronology of Inder Kaur's life, 1911–1996

1911	Inder Kaur is born in Rawalpindi
1911	Her mother, Sant Kaur, dies nine months later
1918	Masi Jasram, the aunt who looked after Inder Kaur, gets married
1920	Nanaji, her maternal grandfather, dies. She moves to her father's house
1924	Taken out of school after completing 8th class
1928	Marries Dr Pargat Singh in Rawalpindi
1929	Lata is born
	Meets Bapuji for the first time
1929, 1930, 1937	Husband has manic episodes
1933	Ranjan is born
1940	Baijee, her stepmother, dies
1941	Husband goes to Iraq
	Inder Kaur completes her BA (Hons) Gyani examnations in Punjabi
1944	Supriya (Kuki) is born
1947, January	Family moves to Karachi
1947, August	Partition of British India
1948	Family moves to Bombay and then to Delhi
	Begins teaching at Queen Mary's School, Delhi
	Passes her matriculation
1950	Passes FA
1952	Passes the English subject for her BA
	Supervises the building of the Nizamuddin house, completed in two and a half months
1955	Passes the History subject for her BA
1955	Completes the full BA with Punjabi, English and History as subjects
1956	Husband leaves home and Inder Kaur moves to the Working Girls' Hostel
1958	Obtains MA in Punjabi literature from the University of Delhi
	Lecturer in Khalsa College, University of Delhi
	Teaches MA students of Punjabi, University of Delhi
1967	Acting Principal, Mata Sundari College for Women, University of Delhi
1969	Founding Principal, Khalsa College for Women, Amritsar
1971	Founding Principal, Lopon College for Women
1976	Founding Principal, Bibi Rajni College, Patti
1977	Begins living in Dharamshala for the summer
1979	Bapuji dies
1986	Retires to settle in Amritsar. Lives in Dharamshala from April to September
1989	Professor Thakur Singh dies, aged 89
1992	Husband dies in Delhi, aged 94
1996	Inder Kaur dies in Amritsar, aged 85

Inder Kaur's Natal Family (*Paikai*)

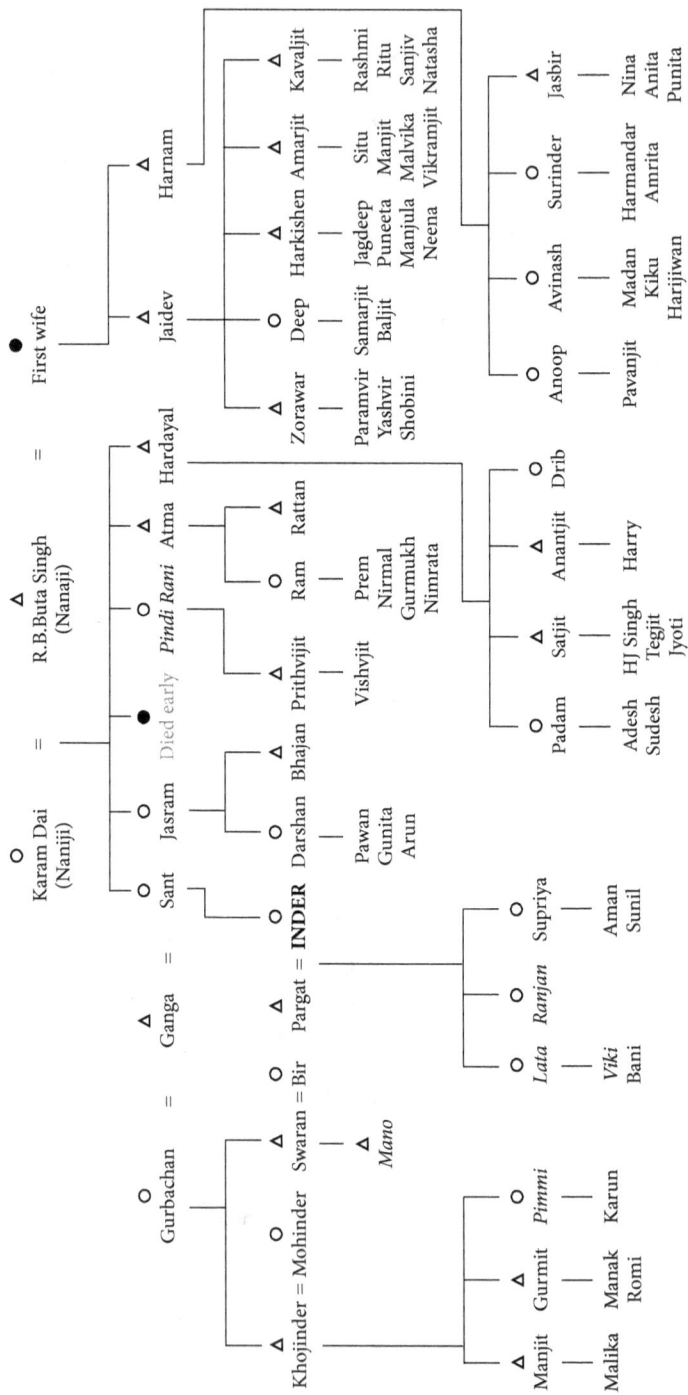

Gurbachan = Ganga = R.B.Buta Singh (Naniji) = First wife
Karam Dai (Naniji)

Khojinder = Mohinder Swaran = Bir Pargat = INDER Sant Jasram *Pindi Rani* Atma Hardayal Jaidev Harnam

Mano

Manjit Gurmit *Pimmi* Lata *Ranjan* Supriya Darshan Bhajan Prithvijit Vishvjit Ram Rattan Zorawar Harkishen Amarjit Kavaljit

Malika Manak Karun *Viki* Aman Pawan Prem Paramvir Jagdeep Situ Rashmi
Romi Bani Sunil Gunita Nirmal Yashvir Puneeta Manjit Ritu
Arun Gurmukh Shobini Manjula Malvika Sanjiv
Nimrata Neena Vikramjit Natasha

Padam Satjit Anantjit Drib Anoop Avinash Surinder Jasbir

Adesh HJ Singh Harry Pavanjit Madan Harmandar Nina
Sudesh Tegjit Kiku Amrita Anita
Jyoti Harijiwan Punita

Bapuji's Family Tree

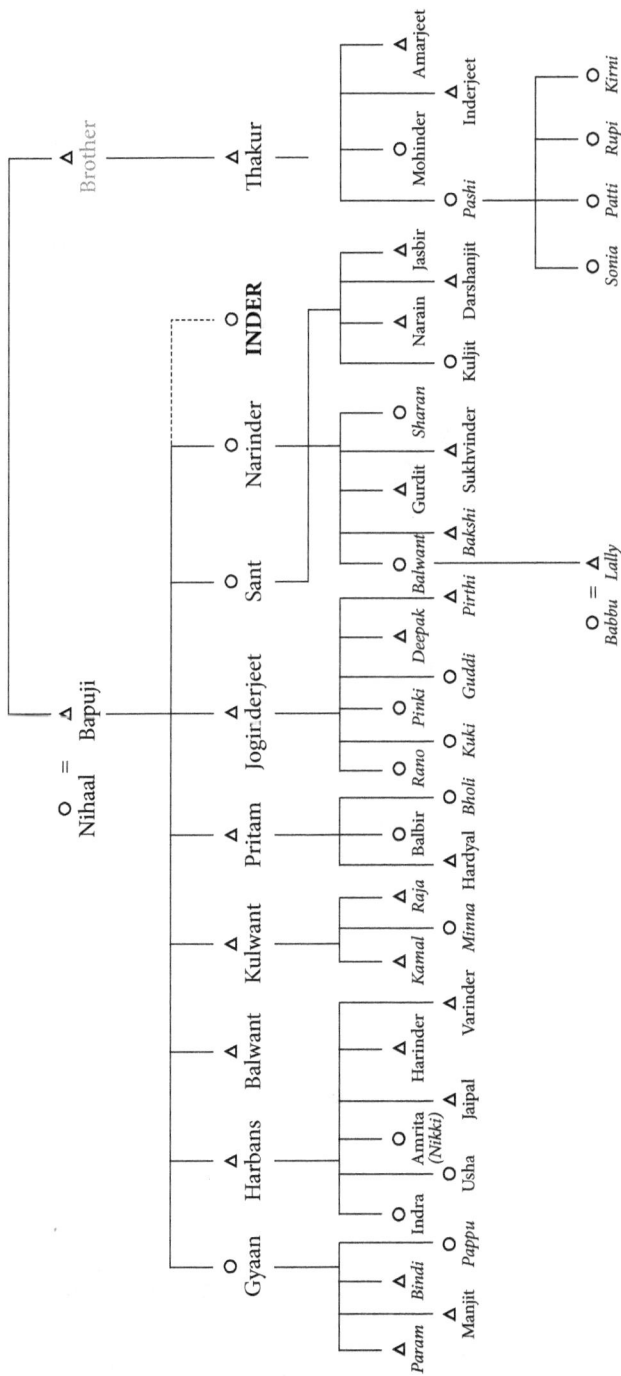

(Nicknames are in italics)

Glossary

Akhand paath	a continuous reading of the Guru Granth Sahib which takes three days
amrit	nectar made from water and sugar, used to initiate Sikhs into a life of truthful living
angithi	cooking stove made with a bucket as the base and formed with mud
ardas	prayer
bagh	thickly embroidered shawl in the traditional Punjabi style
baradari	localised clan grouping
barfi	a sweetmeat made of milk
bata	a round karhai without handles
Bauji	father
Bapuji	father
Bharjaiji	brother's wife
Bhaini	elder sister
Bhuaji	father's sister
Bibi	traditional term of address for young women
burka	the long veil worn by traditional Muslim women in Northern India and Pakistan
Chachaji	father's younger brother
Chidwa	thin rice flakes
coolies	porters
Dadaji	father's father
Dadiji	father's mother
dadkai	home of paternal kin
darshan	coming to pay homage
dastar	a small navy blue turban
diwan	prayer sitting
dholak	rectangular drum beaten on both sides and hung around the neck
dupatta	the long scarf worn with the Punjabi salwar kameez

x

durree	thick cotton woven spread for the bed or the floor
ghara	earthen pot used to store water
gokhrai	heavy gold bracelets
Gurdwara	temple – literally the door of the guru
Gyaniji	a functionary of the Gurdwara
halwai	sweetmeat maker
himmat	courage, energy and daring
hukumnama	the religious reading for the day
iktara	a one-stringed instrument used to accompany hymns
jalebi	spirals of fried batter dunked in syrup
jatha	religious group or sect
jogni	she who meditates on the glory of God
karai	bracelets
kameez	the tunic worn by women as part of traditional Punjabi dress
khes	thick woven bedcloth
kirtan	hymns
langgar	the communal meal in the Gurdwara
lassi	buttermilk
malik	protector
Mamaji	mother's brother
Masiji	mother's sister
Mataji	mother
mem	English woman
misal	one of the 12 territorial Sikh groups that emerged in the 18th century
Nanaji	mother's father
Naniji	mother's mother
nankai	home of maternal kin
nawar	broad woven tape used to weave the base of the bed
nitnem	daily prayers
paath	prayers from the holy book
paikai	a woman's parents' or brother's home as opposed to the home of her in-laws

panjiri	semolina, raisins and nuts roasted in lots of ghee
phalsai	a tart purplish-black fruit
piarai	five men who are seen as beloved of God. They do the Sikh initiation.
Pir	Muslim title of honour given to a religious leader or saint
Pitajee	father
purai	sweet fried puffed wheat bread
puri	fried puffed wheat bread
rani	queen
roti	wheat bread
seer	0.93310 kilogram
shagan	a ritual gift offering of cash
shukar hai	expression of gratitude, literally "Praise be" or "It is good"
simran	a prayer with every breath
tola	ten grammes
virag	a state of desolate religious longing

Acknowledgments

I began this book after my mother's death. I listened to seven hours of her taped memories. I drew on the recollections of others in the family. They would have told a different story because, for the most part, this is a story of the mother I knew, or thought I knew.

The story is worth telling, for my mother was an ordinary woman who achieved extraordinary things. My mother's story is rooted in India, particularly in the Partition of Punjab and its aftermath. Partition shattered my mother's traditional world in Rawalpindi. Pushed to go into paid work in Delhi, she sought an education and then herself became an educator of women. In writing of her life, I wanted to document one Indian woman's struggles during the 20th century for independence, meaning and self worth. She chose the directions of her life but paid a price in that her marriage disintegrated. She achieved financial independence but did not ask herself if she was a feminist. Family and religion remained central, as did some of the patriarchal values of her time.

This is also my story of trying to make sense of my mother's life after living more than half my years in Malaysia and Australia. Because I felt my mother knew me, I thought I knew her and her world. But in the writing of her story I discovered I had thought the part of her life that I had shared was the whole of her life. In connecting with my mother, I too had blanked out the parts of my life that did not resonate with her journey from Rawalpindi to Dharamshala.

The debt to my family who shared their memories with me is evident throughout the book. Anita Anand in India continued to have faith that this is a story worth telling. My thanks to Pat Matsueda who published an excerpt in Mixed Nerve. I also want to thank Indira Sehgal in the United States, who copy edited the draft manuscript. Annette Ryan copy edited the final manuscript and Paul Ryan made it ready for publication. And my thanks to Perle Besserman in Melbourne who saw my story in my mother's.

Chapter 1

Dawn in Dharamshala

I sit in my mother's house in Dharamshala seeing the outer Himalayan ranges glowing in the early morning light. The glow suffuses the low-lying peaks on the right, slowly moving westwards. After an hour-long display, the sun emerges suddenly from behind the mountains. My mother used to sit on the same high divan bed saying, "*Shukar hai, shukar hai*". How do I translate this? Thankfulness is what it means, thankfulness from a grateful heart. To how many is it given to wake up to a view of the Himalayas?

Shukar hai, Shukar hai

My mother also said "*Shukar hai, shukar hai*" when she was sitting in her two-room unit in Amritsar. The cement floor was not quite level, the wiring was suspect, the bathroom was outside the house and pigs rummaged in the garbage heaped by the road. There was a coughing, querulous landlady, nearly always lying on a bed outside my mother's room.

My mother, then 75, would sit on her bed, holding court among her many visitors, dispensing advice to all who came. I asked her once what made her think she could tell people what to do, and she retorted, "I am sitting here. It is they who come." And then the common refrain, "*Shukar hai, shukar hai*". To how many people is it given to have a place of their own and the means to live with freedom and dignity?

My mother's eyesight began to fail when she was 70. When she was 75, she gave up her position as Founding Principal of Bibi Rajni College in Patti, an hour's train ride from Amritsar. She could no longer see the boundaries of objects and so could not read and sign documents. She was thankful she could still see the way.

When I told Mummy in Dharamshala that I had been attacked two months earlier while sleeping in my house in Melbourne and my forehead had been split open, she said, "*Shukar hai, shukar hai*", for I was sitting in front of her, unharmed. She was grateful she had not heard of it two months earlier over the phone. Then she pondered over the strangeness of the fact that a stranger had come into my isolated bush home, picked up an axe from the woodpile, come into my room, beat me on the head and then suddenly run away.

"*Shukar hai, shukar hai*", she said. "The Singhs, the warriors of Guru Gobind Singh Ji must have been protecting you. *Shukar hai, shukar hai*", she said. The next day she offered money for a prayer of thankfulness.

My mother's equanimity failed her for many months before her death, as the family split over a dispute about property in Delhi. Then she thought the way out would be for me to continue renting her unit in the Gurdwara building in Dharamshala after her death. That way I would have a home in India.

I warmed to the idea slowly. Why would I want to come to India after her death? I had spent more than half my life outside India. I had left India for Malaysia when I got married in 1967. After another marriage and divorce, I was single again and living in Melbourne. Even if I came to India, why would I want to leave Delhi? Dharamshala is a small town, pleasant enough, but 12 hours away from Delhi by bus and far from most of the people I know in India.

Summers in Dharamshala

My mother began spending her summers in Dharamshala in 1977, soon after she went to Patti to start the Bibi Rajani College for Women. She came with a colleague who had an uncle in Dharamshala. At first Mummy rented a room. She soon discovered the Gurdwara. The town has a small but enthusiastic Sikh community of about a hundred families, some of whom are refugees from Pakistan. Most of the Sikhs are traders. She gave a talk at the local Gurdwara and soon after, they offered to rent her a unit in the Gurdwara building. She spent the next nine summer holidays in Dharamshala until her retirement. Then for the last ten years of her life, she spent half the year there from April to September.

Dharamshala used to be a sleepy town at the end of the road, nestled below the Dhauladhar ranges of the outer Himalayas, overlooking the Kangra valley. Now in Himachal Pradesh, it used to be part of Punjab and the links continue. Historically, it takes its name from a building that served as a *dharmshal*, a night shelter for travellers. This shelter was built by the Raja of Kangra, Dharam Chand (1528–63), for people who needed to stay overnight to see him at his fort further up the hill at Dharamkot village. However, the main impetus for the town's growth came from 1848 onwards with British settlement. In 1947 when the British left, the town slumped.

Dharamshala gained international recognition in 1959 when India offered political asylum to the 14th Dalai Lama. The Dalai Lama and his people settled in the upper portion of Dharamshala, called McLeod Ganj. Since then, Dharamshala has steadily grown in population and as a destination for tourists and Buddhists. In 2001, the Census listed the population for the Dharamshala Muncipal Area as 19,124. The town is still so small that it is not on all the maps of India. Even the regional radio station does not always give the temperature for Dharamshala.

The town is an interesting mix of hill people (Paharis), Punjabis who came there after Partition (they are still called refugees), those who came from Punjab as tradesmen attracted by its recent growth, and Afghani traders and coolies. Upper Dharamshala, that is, McLeod Ganj, attracts travellers and scholars drawn to the Dalai Lama and Tibetan Buddhism. Visitors to the area also include newly married couples, the brides still wearing their red wedding bangles, who come to visit the shrines to female Hindu deities dotted throughout Himachal Pradesh.

Part of Dharamshala's charm is that it remains a town at the end of the road, fringed by jungle. People talk of panthers and leopards snatching dogs away from the houses at the edge of the jungle. You don't go to Dharamshala on the way to anywhere else. The roads connecting Dharamshala wind down the mountain in hairpin bends. Pathankot is the transport hub and a connecting point to Delhi to the south, Jammu to the north and all the valleys of the Himachal.

Delhi is 526 km away. There is a train from Pathankot to Delhi but it is often late in winter. There is also an air service that connects Delhi and Gaggal, half an hour away from Dharamshala. The only time I used it, because of bad weather, it dropped me off in Kulu, the next valley, eight hours away by taxi. You also can get to Dharamshala by taxi but, travelling alone, my preference remains the night bus. The challenge of bus travel is the toilet stop. I was once faced with a toilet with no light. When I complained to the manager, he said, "Madam, there is a light but there is no bulb." I began travelling with an emergency bag with a torch, soap and toilet paper. The next year when the bus stopped, I went prepared with my toilet bag. There was a palatial hotel at the top of a flight of stairs, with marble floors in the bathroom and the smell of naphthalene.

Dharamshala is a town divided into three by function and population. The District headquarters for the Kangra valley are in Lower Dharamshala (1000 metres above sea level). In the middle is the commercial centre of the town, called Kotwali Bazaar (at 1,250 metres). This is where my mother lived. Kotwali is dominated by an old-style market. Many of the customers are Tibetans and tourists from McLeod Ganj (2,000 metres). I don't know whether my mother ever visited McLeod Ganj. Every now and again the question of meeting the Dalai Lama would come up, but my mother did not consider herself worthy enough.

Dharamshala was my mother's special place. In Amritsar, she was with Bapuji's family (Bapuji was her adopted father). In Delhi she was with her brothers and her daughter. Dharamshala was the place that belonged to her alone. She loved the sight of the mountains. They reminded her of the summers she had spent as a child in Murree, near Rawalpindi, when she would run all day among the hills till she could hear the servants calling for her. Once it was suggested to her that mountains were bad for people with high blood pressure. But my mother became depressed even at the thought of not going there and decided it was worth the risk.

In the 19 years she visited Dharamshala she developed her own family-like network of friends. In the first flat in her row of three flats were Gurmeet and her husband, Gyaniji (a functionary of the Gurdwara), and their son. Gurmeet cooked for Mummy for many months when she did not have a maid. In the flat below were the doctor and his wife. They met every day. That is where we would telephone her before she got a telephone connected. Below that again was Bhaiji, the Head Priest, and his family, a continuous source of support. Then there was the large Mastan Singh clan, originally from Pindi. And Baljeet and his family (Baljeet is the one who got her phone connected, at a time when a connection warranted the distribution of sweets). Jagjit Singh and his wife Bhupinder lived across from the flats. Bhupinder was a teacher and ran the Punjabi school that my mother helped initiate. In Lower Dharamshala there were Tinku, his parents and his wife and children. Tinku and his father ran a general merchandise store in Kotwali Bazar. Tinku was like a son to her. But his mother too felt like a daughter to Mummy.

Mummy came back to the idea of Dharamshala as my base in India. "You can always give it up. And you may want a place to write", she said. Before she died, she had spoken to the Gurdwara Committee, decided on the rent I would pay and formalised the tenancy in her name and mine. When lying ill in Amritsar, she waited for my sister Ranjan to come from New York. She handed the keys to the Dharamshala unit to Ranjan to give to me.

My first visit to Dharamshala

In December 1995, I visited my mother's Dharamshala home for the first time. I generally saw my mother in Delhi or in Amritsar, where she usually spent the winter. But in 1995 she had decided to winter in Dharamshala. She came with Tinku in a taxi to the station near Pathankot, three hours away from Dharamshala, to pick me up. They had to wait a couple of hours, for the train was late starting in the Delhi winter fog. At nearly 85, she was having difficulty walking and the wait told on her.

My mother had made a cosy home of the three-room unit below the Gurdwara. Her unit was part of a four-storey building built into the hillside below the Gurdwara. There were three flats to a floor joined by a common corridor. The house was painted ochre with windows and doors in blue, a colour scheme repeated throughout the region.

Her bed was in the front room with a direct view of the Dhauladhar ranges. It was a box bed made by Sukhdev, a local carpenter. She stored the quilts in it during the summer. This room was also the living room, so in the morning the bed became a divan where she would sit cross-legged, with a bolster at her back. A covered iron trunk was on one side, holding some of the photographs important to her. Most of them were of her and Bapuji's family. The only photograph of her with her nuclear family was one that showed my two sisters flanking my mother and father, sitting apart on sofa chairs. Seeing that there was none of me, I framed the photograph I had sent her earlier of my doctoral graduation. There was also a plaque given to her as Principal of Khalsa College for Women in Amritsar. That was the only sign in the room that she was an educator, that she had started three women's colleges in Punjab.

Her identity in Dharamshala was focused on religion and family – with most of the visiting family coming from Bapuji's family in Punjab rather than Delhi. For a while, people knew her as the Patti Principal, referring to her last college in Patti, near Amritsar. But towards the end, before she died in March 1996, she was known as Mataji (Mother). She seemed to be their mother rather than mine. Even in the few days I spent with her in Dharamshala, I kept trying to get my mother back, the one who would spar with me intellectually.

There was a bed along another wall in her room, against the window. That is where I sat, huddled in a quilt to see the winter dawn, and where we talked before visitors arrived. The valley lay below, past the paper kites impaled on trees and electric wires. Both beds were covered by pink bedspreads given by Darshan Masi, the cousin who was closest to her. On the floor was a pink carpet that had seen better days. On top of that was an elegant red carpet with a central floral pattern, a present to her from my sisters and me. She had waited for me to come to choose thicker curtains which would be suitable for winter. She also needed new rattan chairs from Kangra, she said.

Directly outside the bedroom door was a large cotton painting from Indonesia, in orange and blue of serpents churning the water. When Mummy visited us in Kuala Lumpur in 1982, she liked it and my younger son Sunil gave it to her.

I slept in the inner room with two beds and a dressing table. She had gone with a friend in a taxi to get a new cotton mattress for my bed. The room otherwise was much the same as the front room, but with a view of the valley instead of the mountains.

In the hallway was a carved dining table with fluted legs. The kitchen was custom-made for one person. There was a gas table-top stove on one concrete shelf. Another two storage shelves above held the brass and stainless steel pots, the stainless steel *thalis*, bowls, plates and spoons. The rice and flour were in large plastic bins. The rolling pin and board to make the *chapatis* were there too. In the cupboard to the left were the lentils, spices, oil and pickles. There was no sink, for the dishes were washed on the floor using a tap below the shelves.

Swarna, a 16-year-old girl from a nearby village, looked after my mother. She stayed in the back room whose walls she had plastered with magazine prints of film actors. Her room is now my study.

I had to learn how to have a bath again in the style of my childhood. The electric coiled heating rod was clamped to a rough piece of wood that went across a plastic bucket containing the bathwater. Twenty minutes later, the water was hot. Sitting on a wooden stool, I bathed from the bucket using a mug as a dipper. There was no running water, for the water was only expected twice a day at 6 a.m. and 6 p.m. The toilet was modern, specially installed because with her bad knees my mother could not squat on the traditional style toilet.

As in Amritsar, people began streaming in as the winter sun moved towards my mother's unit. When one lot went, another group came, and my mother would say, "Come, come. Blessed is our fortune that you have come. I haven't seen you all day. Come, come. Let us have tea." Swarna would begin to brew the tea. It was not like the tea we made in Delhi – tea, water and a bit of milk. Here, it was brewed for a while with cardamom and cloves, and with nearly as much milk as water. "Bring out the dry fruit", she said. Before one neighbour left, another came. "Come in, come in, welcome", my mother would chant. "Put the tea on", she would tell Swarna. "Come, come. Sit, sit. You make my heart feel glad."

Some came to see me to honour Mataji, and also to check out this Australian daughter. The litany would begin. When did you arrive? Where do you stay? But soon the conversation went back to the familiar tracks – life in Dharamshala, births, marriages and death, matters of religion.

In the afternoon, the doctor's wife, who lived below, came as was her routine. Again the same questions. Gurmeetji, who lived in the corner flat, came to call. She wore the *dastar*, the headgear distinctive of the sect to which my mother belonged. Then Bhupinder, the teacher who lived across from the flats, came with her daughter-in-law. "How many children do you have?" she asked. "What does your *sardarji* (husband) do?" I told her I was divorced. "I am so sorry", she said. The questions stopped.

My mother later told me there was no need to be so direct. "What should I say?" I asked.

"Go roundabout, go roundabout, be vague."

"How roundabout can you get?" I asked. "At least I did not say I was divorced twice, and that one husband is in Malaysia and the other has remarried in Tasmania."

It was a delicious situation. Was this daughter going to ruin her mother's reputation? We spent the rest of the evening laughing. "Neither of us made good wives", my mother said. "We have always done what we wanted."

Not everybody came at once. Bhaiji's daughter-in-law, who lived downstairs, did not appear for two days. "What happened?" my mother asked. Bharjaiji (brother's wife) – that is what I came to call her – said:

I was shy. I did not know what big sister would be like, for she lives abroad. Maybe she is a *mem* [an English woman]. I thought maybe she does not speak Punjabi and then what would I say? But

I could not resist coming up. For the last two days, I have been hearing laughter day and night, and I came up to see.

Bhaiji came every morning to ask what he should get for my mother from the market. My mother could not go herself, and the market was not seen as a fit place for Swarna at the age of 16. At 67, Bhaiji was upright in bearing, with a flowing white beard, dressed in a white *kurta* and pyjama and blue turban. He has remained my main source of support in Dharamshala; he is the person who pays my bills, who ensures that the rent is paid, who gets the electrician and the telephone man to come if the monkeys cut the wires while I am away.

The milkman came, asking how much milk we wanted that day. A discussion followed with Swarna to check whether we needed milk for curd, whether we were going to have rice pudding that night or grated carrot *halwa*.

Later in the morning, Swarna brought Bhaiji's two-year-old granddaughter Arzoo to get her daily gift of rock sugar. Bhaiji's two grandsons came with their final exam results and Mummy gave them Rs 5 each. Soon we saw two kites in the sky. The grandsons came throughout the day – just to return a pot, a plate, bring some delicacies from their mother or to keep an eye on news as it was developing.

Every now and again, the sounds of the vegetable man selling spinach, carrots and turnips would float up. "Do we need more vegetables?" my mother would ask Swarna. Sometimes a carpet man would haul carpets up to the flat hoping for a sale. Men came by on bicycles and Bhaiji's grandsons would come running up to ask whether we needed our knives sharpened, pressure cooker repaired, keys made.

Sukhdev, the carpenter, came to replace the mottled glass in the front window with clear glass so that we could see the mountains clearly. My mother said, "All these years I have been craning my neck to see the mountains from the side." The bars on the windows and the wire clothesline strung between the pillars remained. In the middle of all this, red-bottomed monkeys thundered onto the roof and grouped on the right side of the verandah. "Run, run", everybody would shout. "Close the doors. Close the doors. Have they run off with the bananas?"

The visiting did not stop at night. After dinner, my mother's next door neighbour, an engineer, came by. His wife was visiting from the village where she taught and had brought special things to eat. Even when the electricity went off there were visitors, for every house had candles on hand. This was, of course, a time before the neighbourhood got colour TV and cable.

In the early morning and late at night when we were alone, my mother talked of her thankfulness that she could hear so acutely. "I pleaded with God", she said, "to let me continue to hear so that I could hear His name." As it became more difficult for her to walk, the Gurdwara upstairs piped the morning hymns to her room via a special speaker. The scriptures she already knew in her head – the result of a lifetime of religious devotion and a critical study of religious poetry for her master's degree in Punjabi literature.

Her day began at 4 a.m. when the hymns from the Golden Temple in Amritsar are broadcast on the radio. By that time she would have had her bath, except for particularly cold mornings when she said God understood. Or days when we had talked late into the night.

In Dharamshala, as in Delhi and Amritsar, we talked of her life and mine. Each time we met, we needed to re-establish the small talk that could not be communicated by letter or phone. Also to say the things we could not say to anybody else. We talked of death. We were conscious that it might be the last time we were to meet. It was a distinct possibility, with me in Melbourne and she in Dharamshala. Staying in Dharamshala, she had also accepted that when the time of her death came she would be far away from her daughter and brothers in Delhi.

She talked of the way Charan, my first husband, had come to offer his condolences to her in Delhi when my father died, how he had acknowledged family ties, that his children's grandfather had died. Then, changing tack, she said, "Who would have thought that Charan would lend you money to buy your house after your second divorce?

When God wants to help, he pulls down the pillars and helps."

It was a time to count our blessings. As soon as my youngest son, Sunil, went to university, for the first time I asked myself what I wanted to do. This led me to university in Melbourne to do my doctoral degree. I went back to sociology and a life of writing and scholarship. I had good friends who had been with me when I was alone. I talked of my pleasure in my Melbourne home among the gum trees and the birds. I needed to describe my life in Melbourne in detail, for she said she would not be able to visit. Even if her knees held out during the 13-hour journey, she would not be able to manage the cramped airplane toilets.

So I described my house high on a hill, with its cathedral ceilings, the 100-year-old wood inside and outside the house, looking out on a forest of eucalyptus trees. I told her of my delight in the large rolling garden. The yellow wattle I had planted along the drive made winter a blaze of yellow. There were white and mauve agapanthus along the driveway and a cascade of yellow jasmine falling over the rock wall. The geraniums provided a bank of colour. I tried to tell her of the red hot pokers in my garden, bright orange spikes in the summer, and the purple buddlea. There was of course the red and pink callistemon that was also seen along the tea gardens in Dharamshala. I was planting plums and apricots, nectarines and peaches, lemons and olive trees. There was also a quince tree and a stream running below that I could see from the kitchen and from the large deck surrounding the living room.

I described to her the smell of the eucalyptus after the rain, the sound of the wind chimes hanging outside the kitchen. I told her of the birds that came every day, often the only visitors. Most of the time it was pigeons, including the bronze-winged pigeons, which glinted in the sun. There were kookaburras nesting in the large gum tree outside the kitchen. The red, blue and green rainbow lorikeets came in groups, chattering away. The large white and yellow sulphur-crested cockatoos visited and I had learnt to be wary of their destructive ways with wood. Twice a year flocks of yellow-tailed cockatoos visited but never came too near. I knew them by their distinctive call. When the hawthorn berries were ripe, *gang-gangs* got drunk on them. They were black cockatoos with touches of red and grey. There were also pink galahs. "Why don't we have a bird feeder here?" I asked. "The monkeys will come", she reminded me.

She talked of her love for her grandfather, for Bapuji, for Professor Thakur Singh – Bapuji's nephew and her soul mate – and she talked of the joys of education and her comfort in religion. "I am waiting for death", she said. "I am waiting at the station but the whistle does not blow." We collapsed into laughter. This was something she could not choreograph.

"That's very well for you", I said, "but what will happen to me?"

"The spirits look after those they love", she said.

"Well, in that case, here is my wish list for when you have greater power to deliver", and we laughed again.

"There is no need to rush back for the cremation", she said seriously, for every visit was also a goodbye. "The body just becomes a heap of ashes. Come for the prayers, for it is the spirit that matters."

Mummy and I – our last photograph together, January 1996

My mother died three months later, after a brief illness in Amritsar. I arrived in time for the prayers. Mirroring her life, the main prayers were held in Amritsar. After a memorial service in Delhi, my sister

Ranjan and I came to Dharamshala to organise an *akhand paath*, the three-day continuous reading of the Sikh holy book, the Guru Granth Sahib. One by one, Mummy's neighbours and friends came, not to commiserate with us in our grief but to mourn her for themselves. People streamed in to talk of my mother. All of them said how she had loved them in a special way, how she was the mother or sister they had never had. They did not talk of her achievements. They talked of the love she had given them. They were the chief mourners, we the outsiders. "Don't think", one of her neighbours said, "that if you had not come to hold the prayers, there would have been no prayers said for *Mataji*." And in the overflowing hall where prayers were chanted for three continuous days and nights, it was announced that the congregation would hold another *akhand paath* in the monsoon months.

Writing of my mother
In Dharamshala, I find myself trying to repeat part of my mother's routine, as if that will bring her back. I wake up before dawn, heat a bucket of water with an electric rod. I make some cereal that has been locally ground and roasted, and drink tea that I have brewed with a quarter cup of milk in a stainless steel glass. I make sure that I fill the large red and blue plastic buckets with water, not forgetting the smaller buckets in the bathroom, kitchen, toilet and near the sink in the hallway. If the pressure is good, some water will be left over to fill the black plastic tank that sits on wooden supports below the roof of the bathroom. I breakfast as the sun rises over the Dhauladhar ranges, go to the Gurdwara at 7.45 for half an hour.

In the first few years I go to the Buddhist Dharma classes at the Tibetan library, if they are on. Going slowly up the mountain, I barely make it before 9 a.m. when the chanting begins. There the lesson of the day is about laziness as one of the causes of suffering. One kind of laziness is putting things off for another day. I come back and start writing again.

My mother and I had assumed that one day I would write about her. In 1986, ten years before she died, I had taped my mother telling her story on seven one-hour tapes. I was preparing for her death. As a sociologist and historian, I also wanted to record history as it was being played out in my family.

My mother tells her story chronologically on tape: her mother's death soon after she was born, her early years in her grandfather's house, adjusting to life with a stepmother, marriage, coming to terms with a manic-depressive husband, the happiness of being a mother, the joy of religious experience and finding a new family with Bapuji. Then there was Partition, the search for education, the disintegration of her marriage and the achievement of financial independence.

At one level my mother's story is the story of the subservient status of women in the India of the first half of the 20th century and of the social change hastened by Partition in 1947. In my mother's story, which began in 1911, women typically died before their menfolk. They died of childbirth, of tuberculosis, of stomach aches, of undiagnosed fevers. It was assumed the women would eat after the men and eat less. They also were given only a few years of schooling, if any. My mother's father was not unusual in the Punjab of the 1920s in withdrawing his daughter from school after she reached puberty.

My mother lived through tumultuous times in Punjab: the Ghadar movement and the Gurdwara Reform Movement of the early 20th century, the Jalianwalah Bagh massacre of 1919, and the Civil Disobedience and Quit India movements of 1930 and 1942. She did not speak of them, other than to mention in passing that she had once shouted the slogan for the Akali party in school but was stopped. This silence was remarkable, not only because these were some of the most important years in the formation of modern India, but because there were male family connections with many of these events. Bhai Randhir Singh, the head of the religious sect to which my mother and father belonged, was one of the first freedom fighters of Punjab. He was the first prisoner of the Gurdwara Reform movement and was in jail from May 1915 to October 1930. Professor Thakur Singh was at Jalianwala Bagh on 13 April 1919 when General Dyer instructed soldiers to shoot at the assembled peaceful crowd of some 20,000 people.

This silence troubled me until I found her silence itself evocative.

The only women who are mentioned in connection with the struggle for independence in Punjab are women of royal lineage like Rajkumari Amrit Kaur, the wives of advocates involved in the Civil Disobedience Movement like Pushpa Gujral and Amar Kaur, or widows like Budhwati, Harnam Kaur and Channo Devi. The political history of Punjab has been written by men. For my mother, as for many women of the middle class, her world until 1947 was the world of the home, family, kin and religion. It was as a result of Partition, rather than Independence, that the political events of the time came crashing into her life.

Partition was the backdrop of every story I heard as I was growing up. Whenever anyone asked my mother where she came from, she used to say, "Pindi". The Punjabi she spoke was recognised as the language of Rawalpindi, the chickpea dish she made was from a recipe from a corner shop in Pindi, the local residential clan group, the *baradari*, was from Pindi.

Fortunately, in our home Partition was more a story to be told than a sorrow to be endured. Contrary to everything that has been written about Partition in history books and literature, for my mother it had been a liberating experience. With Partition had come the necessity and opportunity for employment. It became possible to pursue her dream of getting an education. For my father, Partition meant the end of a world that revolved around the unquestioned authority of the husband. It was he who in this new world loomed as the tragic figure.

This was the story, or at least part of it. I found the telling of it more difficult. At first, the outpouring was my cry in the loneliness of grief in Melbourne where nobody knew my mother. I then tried to tell my mother's story in different voices. I asked others in my family to tell their stories of the same events. To ground myself, I tried to place my mother's story within the history of women in Punjab. But I could not find my mother's voice in much of the history that is written. I went to Lahore and Rawalpindi to try to get a feel for the physical context of my mother's story. As I walked the streets, I realised that my mother's story of Pindi was not the story of a city but the story of kin. A connected local kinship network had existed in Pindi. This was not the case for us in Delhi. My mother had managed to recreate some of it with Bapuji's family in Amritsar and Tarn Taran, and to construct a make-believe version of it in Dharamshala.

The story sputtered. At the centre of my story of my mother lay her struggle for education and freedom. But as I wrote, I discovered that religion had been at the centre of her life. Bound with her religious quest was her love for Bapuji, her adopted father, and Professor Thakur Singh, his nephew. Religion was the dominant force in her young adult life and these new relationships gave her another family and another love.

Her knowledge of the scriptures fed into a critical study of Gurbani for her Master's degree in Punjabi literature. She returned to religion as the main theme of her last ten years. She had told me this, but I had not understood, for it had little resonance with my own life. Now that I myself have questions about religion, I wish my mother were still here. Having known her mix of devotion and academic knowledge, I find it hard to sit at somebody else's feet.

The mother I knew who sought education and became an educator was different from the housewife my sisters knew when they were growing up in Pindi. Our mother the devotee was a mother that none of us knew.

It was dispiriting to recognise I knew so little of my mother's life. I always thought she knew me and my story. When talking to her, it was as if I found myself. I had lived with her for only 23 years in Karachi and Delhi, a bit more than one-fourth of her life. I knew the small part of her life that I had shared and had thought it was the whole. However, so much had happened to her before I was born and after I left India. I could listen to what she said, but did not have the questions that would have probed her silences. I had asked her some questions, but the significance of others has only become apparent in the process of writing. In the end I began to feel that perhaps actually the story lay in the gaps and the silences.

I wondered then if I also only talked of the part of my life I could share with my mother, and neither of us knew the silent expanses of the other. When I left for Malaysia, I had withdrawn into my own silences. I could talk about the flowers in my father-in-law's garden, the kindness of my grandmother-in-law, my pleasure in my children. But it was difficult to convey the loneliness of a bad marriage, of life without money of my own and the fear that I was sinking into a suicidal mindlessness that even the children might not dispel. In this blankness I had failed to realise the significant changes taking place in my mother's life.

I thought this kind of disconnection was something that happened most dramatically with migrants, when whole aspects of their lives do not click into perspective in their new country. But the past – particularly in my mother's case where there was so much discontinuity – is also like another country.

I had seen my mother in relation to myself. When I put her at the centre, the story changed. And so I wrote again, but at first only in Dharamshala. It was as if the daily realities of the small town where she had spent her last nineteen summers grounded me, giving me a feel for the years that I did not know at first hand. She had been happy here, surrounded by friends who were like kin.

The three weeks a year I spend in Dharamshala are becoming an important part of my life, giving me a sense of community and a slower pace. I live a simpler life. In Delhi, I can hardly wait to get to Dharamshala. Mama Swaran, my uncle with whom I used to stay in Delhi, grumbled that I ran off to Dharamshala after only two or three days. For me Dharamshala has a sense of a time apart. It is as if I am trying to make myself over, trying to fit into my mother's pattern of life, into readings of religion and philosophy. But after the euphoria of the first two weeks, I begin to look forward to Delhi, even with its traffic hassles, the cold and the fog. In Delhi, after the shock of the high expense of living wears off, I slip easily into the everyday luxuries of my family's lives. I expect hot water from the tap; I go easily in the chauffeured car, while grumbling about the traffic jam. I dress more elegantly, wearing the shawls I have collected from different parts of India. But even in Delhi, I begin to hanker for the rest of me, for my life in Melbourne as a sociologist and to again connect with my son and grandchildren, to dine with my friends and feel I have come home.

When this restlessness overtakes me in Dharamshala I wander in the Himachal to discover an India that I do not know. As the time for goodbye comes closer, I again am entranced by the friendship and community of my neighbours, by their ready acceptance of me just because I am Mataji's daughter. I wonder whether this had also happened to Mummy. Once she admitted she missed the intellectual discussions of the philosophy of Sikhism and the different interpretations of Gurbani. She remembered these from her academic life and she also had some of this in Amritsar. But her Amritsar family visited her often in Dharamshala, so she remained connected. For the most part she was content to recognise the love that was being offered to her in Dharamshala. So perhaps her worlds in Amritsar, Delhi and Dharamshala were more connected than I had thought. I recognise the difference, and begin writing also in Melbourne.

Coming back to Dharamshala

"*Sat Sri Akal Ji, Sat Sri Akal*", says Daljeet, my neighbour, in the traditional Sikh greeting. "You have come. We were expecting you two hours earlier, at 6 a.m. Have you come alone?" Daljeet came to live in the next door flat, where the engineer used to live, after Mummy died. I have known her now for 14 winters in Dharamshala.

"You have come", says Bharjaiji, Bhaiji's daughter-in-law. "You must have your tea and meals with us. Why start your kitchen for three weeks, just for one person?"

The flat has been locked for a year, not counting the day my cousin spent in it. I see the curtains have made it through another monsoon, but the closing-up-the-house bed covers and the *durree* on the floor defeat me. I don't immediately go into the other two rooms and the kitchen. I also do not look up to the Dhauladar ranges and the eagles circling overhead. However, I move Daljeet's washing so that it does not obstruct my view of the mountains. "The snow came on time", says Daljeet.

Arzoo, now nearly 16, Bhaiji's granddaughter, and Jaswinder,

Daljeet's 13-year-old daughter, come to visit. They are now too grown-up to paste welcome posters on my door. I remember one which had a large Mickey Mouse on it saying "Welcome" and on the other they wrote, "Open the door with a smile". Bablu, Arzoo's 23-year-old brother, received me at the bus stand and helped carry my bags the five minutes to the Gurdwara. He is at an in-between stage, waiting for a job to appear and weighing up a decision to do a BA by correspondence. He needs to present himself as an eligible candidate to the parents of the girl he hopes to marry.

Daljeet's husband says that recently there hasn't been a problem with the water. The neighbours downstairs are on leave, so the pressure is strong. This is good news for the water comes at 7 in the morning if it comes on at all. Another water connection may work at 9 a.m. for half an hour or so. Some years, even when the rains have been good, there is something wrong with the pipes. The rains have been sparse, so my neighbours are preparing for an extreme water shortage in the summer. They fear the water may come for an hour once every three days and even the water pump will go dry.

"Do you want milk?" the milkman asks, coming soon after.

"Where is your father?" I ask, seeing the young man.

"Father is at home."

I rinse out the stainless steel pot. "One kilo?" the milkman asks. It is only a few days later when the curd does not set that I realise his milk has become thinner over the years.

Gurmeetji in the farthest unit – she was a friend of my mother's – has asked Kanta, the woman who has been cleaning her house for the last 19 years, to come and see me. Kanta has been helping me with the cleaning, dishes and washing for the last few years in Dharamshala,

I put the mattresses and quilts to air, sweep the floor of the living room cum bedroom. It is perfunctory but will do till Kanta cleans it again. I take out the photographs to place on the tin trunk and the carpet to replace the *durree* on the floor. I shake the pillows that I have had redone after having the cotton respun. The Tibetan cushion spreads go on the cane chairs. I put the batteries back in the radios. Slowly the room begins to take shape. By this time, Bharjaiji has brought up a glass of tea, reminding me to come down for breakfast.

Bhaiji, now 81, comes up after the temple service to make sure I am settled in. He is beginning to look frail. He notes that the telephone is not working, that the window in the second bedroom needs fixing. I ask about his son, Arzoo and Bablu's father, who has moved to Chamba, a Himalayan valley to the north. He is still there as the priest in the Sikh temple. We laugh at our incredulity when the transformation took place from his son driving buses to becoming a respected priest, seven years ago. Bharjaijee, Bhaiji's daughter-in-law, is still in Dharamshala. She cannot leave for Chamba for at least a year, while Arzoo finishes her schooling. If and when she goes, the problem will be to find someone to look after Bhaiji's household in Dharamshala. For over 30 years, Bhaiji's wife has lived in Jammu, looking after the lands and the family of her eldest son. Bhaiji does not seem to be concerned.

There is enough water for a bath. I find the electric heating rod and clip it to a stick that sits across the plastic bucket. First, though, I have to unplug the fridge, for the wiring cannot take two gadgets at the same time. The water gets hot in 20 minutes, and I am ready to go downstairs to Bharjaiji's house for lunch.

After lunch, Arzoo and Jaswinder come back to my flat. When they were in primary school, they used to come for English conversation classes and toffees at 5 p.m. These classes started the year after my mother's death. Like my mother, I looked at Bhaiji's grandsons' exam results and gave them Rs 10 each. Noticing they were weak in English, I told them to come to me every evening. They soon stopped coming, but the class size grew to about 15 and then diminished. Now most of those children are in universities and a new interested batch has yet to emerge.

After lunch I first go to make a condolence call at Raja's computer shop, for his mother, Bhupinder Bhainji, died a few months ago. We talk and cry for a while. She was an important part of the community and of my life in Dharamshala. I then go up the hill to the market to get flour and spices from the man who has a grinding wheel.

"*Sat Sri Akal*", a neighbour across the building says. "When did you come?"

"Just this morning."

"Is everything well? Is your family well?"

"Yes. And is everything well with you?"

"Did you come alone?" she asks.

This becomes a refrain, for in previous years my friends or my sons and daughters-in-law had come with me for a time.

I greet the shopkeeper to the left who has a ration shop. On the same side are the cobbler and his son. They once made a pair of shoes for me. The shop is much expanded. "When did you come? Is everything well?"

I don't see the shop or the man who sold me the sink for the kitchen. Then I pass by the silversmith. "*Namaste, namaste.* When did you come?"

The road has been dug up to put in some pipes. Nobody knows when it will be fixed. At the top of the road is Tinku's general merchandise store. "*Sat Sri Akal*", I greet Tinku. His father is no longer well enough to sit in the shop. Tinku lights up, saying, "When did you come? You came alone?" I ask after his daughter Enu, who has completed her Masters degree in Kathak dancing in Chandigarh. She and I are friends and spend a lot of time together. I tell him I had tried to call, but he says his landline no longer works.

Around the bend is Amrit, who keeps a textile store. Once she had to vouch to the bank that I was who I said I was. She is deep in conversation with another woman. "*Sat Sri Akal*", I say, getting her attention. I tell her I came this morning. Yes, I came alone.

I finally reach the man with the grinding wheel. His shop is at the edge of Kotwali Bazaar – my part of Dharamshala – on the road that connects with the path up the hill to Macleod Ganj, where most of the Tibetans live. He is a wizened old man, gnome-like. After an accident a few years ago, he now hobbles with a stick. I made friends with him when I used to take the path to the Tibetan Library to attend classes on Buddhist philosophy. He once shooed monkeys away from the path so that I could continue up the hill.

"You haven't been for a long time", he upbraids me. "Only a year", I remonstrate. He now wants to be reminded where I live when I am not in Dharamshala. He registers it is Australia, but there is no comment. He packs the kilo of roasted wheat cereal which is freshly ground. He then gives me warm wheat flour for the *chapatis*, telling me I will be able to tell the difference between his flour and the one that is milled.

"That is why I come to you", I tell him.

Then it is the small amounts of spices that will take me through the three weeks I am in Dharamshala.

"What about the *sattu*?" I ask him. I had experimented with it last year. This is roasted wheat, gram and maize flour, much loved by the Tibetans. My memories of *sattu* are connected with Bapuji's family coming from Tarn Taran, bringing *sattu* to drink in the summer. But my spice and flour man tells me I should put a bit of milk and sugar into the *sattu* and make it into balls. A bit of *ghee* in it would be good too.

On the way home, I buy one and a half kilos of radish with leaves for Rs 10. I also stop by the best bakery in town to get cake rusks and assorted freshly baked biscuits. The owner does not recognise me.

I pass by the Public Call Office (PCO) I used to use for long-distance calls. The price would show up on the meter. Now I use my mobile.

My neighbours come in the evening and sit in my study, the small room that used to be Swarna's. She is married now and has a child but no longer visits. Bhaiji had the room repainted to remove traces of the pictures of film stars. I have moved the dining table with the fluted legs into this study. Behind it is a *bagh* that my sister Ranjan gave me. On the floor is a blue *durree* with a red border, flanked by a pile of trunks covered with a smaller blue *durree*. Also in the room is a chair with a blue iron and white formica frame that I have rewoven with white and pink *nawar*. A one-bar heater makes the small study so cosy that this is where people come to visit me once the sun has set. My life and work in Melbourne recede as we talk of Dharamshala – who died, who is ill, who got married and whose children have gone to university. They leave and I begin to write.

Chapter 2

Nanaji

————

My mother was nine months old when her mother died of tuberculosis. The photograph in Delhi of her mother in a silver frame shows a soulful woman with my mother's eyes and lips, wearing a heavy choker and long earings down to her neck.

Mummy's mother, Sant Kaur

The big house

For my mother, her story began with *Nanaji*, her mother's father, Rai Bahadur Buta Singh. Her time with him was bound in an aura of happiness. She kept his photograph in a large frame either hanging on the wall or by her bed, together with her mother's photograph. It was the picture of a man more than six feet tall and broad of build. In the photograph, he wears the medals that came with the British title of Rai Bahadur. He wears a turban – an ordinary turban – without the fantail common in those parts. His beard is open. The silk open coat that covers his knees is trimmed with gold. Underneath the coat he wears a long-sleeved tunic and pyjamas that hug the legs. And on his feet are the gold embroidered shoes typical of Punjab.

Whenever Mummy spoke of her childhood with her grandfather, she glowed. In the one-room unit we rented in a bungalow in Lodhi Estate in Delhi when I was nine, Mummy would talk of Nanaji's three-storey house in Rawalpindi. She would talk of the Big House, of two kinds of horse-driven carriages, and of servants shaking the plum and apricot trees in the family orchards two or three miles outside the city.

She would talk of summers in Nanaji's house in Murree, a hill resort near Pindi, where she would run in the hills, of special maids for each grandchild, of such an abundance of sweets, fruit and milk that she would hanker for the everyday *chapati* she got in her father's house when she went to visit.

Nanaji, Rai Bahadur Buta Singh

Talking of the Big House when she was 75, she remembers its layout – the factories and offices on the ground floor, the brick stairs she would race up and down, the wood-fired stoves in the kitchens, the lavatories on the roof, the woven six-foot fan that cooled the afternoons.

"I remember all the rooms. Everything I remember", she says. There was beautiful Kashmiri carved wood furniture in the living room. "It got left behind in Pakistan. A lot got left behind", she says softly. She continues:

The riches were of the old fashioned kind. We used to wear good clothes. We used to have milk, curds, butter, cream. Crates of fruit would come from orchards in Kashmir. There were almonds, pistachios, pine nuts. Nanaji would bring sweets home. There was a lot to eat. I have seen a lot of wealth. That is why my mind is full.

It was a house full of retainers. Mummy had a special maid called Gurma, whose family used to work for Naniji, Mummy's maternal grandmother. There was a cook, a fan man, a watchman and another two maids. There was another servant whose wife combed Mummy's grandmother's hair and plaited it in fine braids. She also helped her with the bath. There were other maids who massaged the children when they were tired.

The barber came to trim their nails. The gardener brought fruit and vegetables from the land. The milkman brought milk in big earthen pots, while the buffaloes stood outside.

Mummy knew she was the centre of her grandfather's life. "He would tell me, 'The big Santo has gone away, and she has given us the small one'. I did not understand who this Santo was. Later, I found out my mother's name was Sant Kaur."

Nanaji would always bring some kind of sweet delicacy to give to my mother to distribute to the other children. He openly showed that she was his favourite grandchild. When my mother spoke about Nanaji, she spoke of the occasions when he made her feel important and loved, as if continuing to savour them for herself. The story I liked best was the time Nanaji had a swimming pond specially dug for her.

Mummy had wanted to swim in the irrigation tank in the orchard. Nanaji feared it was too deep and so forbade her. A fortnight later he took her to the orchard and showed her a new shallow swimming pond and told her, "You wanted to swim. Now swim."

When Mummy told her story, she talked of how Nanaji would wake her up early in the morning to spoon almonds and cream into her mouth, then let her go back to sleep. When her uncles, her mother's two brothers, got married, Mummy told Nanaji the girls in her school had complained they had not received sweetmeats. He said, "Really?" Next day at noon the family servants brought baskets of sweets to the school. Nanaji had ordered the sweets on his way to work at 4 a.m.. "Happiness permeated through me", my mother said, "that I was so important that something I said to him yesterday, he had fulfilled today."

At the marriages of these uncles, Nanaji had had two gold bangles of five tolas (50g) each made for every granddaughter. Mummy was six or seven years old and somebody took them off her when she was asleep. Afraid of her husband's anger, Naniji did not tell him. Many days passed. Then Nanaji fell ill. When the carriage came to take the children to see him, Nanaji noticed that the other granddaughters wore their bangles but Mummy's arms were bare.

He asked her, "Where are your bangles?"

"I was sleeping and somebody took them off. They have been lost for a long time."

"These devils have bangles and my daughter doesn't?" he said.

He called my mother's father's younger brother and told him to take her to the family jeweller to have bangles made. "And day after tomorrow bring her wearing the bangles", he said. When she came back with the bangles, he held her hand tightly and kissed the bangles and said, "How can my daughter not have bangles?"

Rai Bahadur Buta Singh

Nanaji had received the title of Rai Bahadur for work done for the British. He was a large government contractor for swords, *nawars* (broad, heavy cotton tapes for making beds) and tents. It is said he equipped a whole battalion at his own expense. However, he was not noted as being among the seven main chiefs and families of note in the Rawalpindi district in a compilation done in 1940. For my mother, though, Nanaji stood for all that was rich and noble in her life.

My mother did not question her pride in Nanaji's title. There was no hint that in an independent India her grandfather could have been seen as a collaborator. He was like the other better known Ahluwalias of the Kapurthala dynasty, known for their support of the British during the First World War. My mother saw the title as due recognition for a self-made man who was generous, compassionate, charitable. He built schools and Sikh temples, helped orphans and widows, gave blankets to the poor, fed holy men. Mummy was particularly touched to see his name inscribed among the donors for Khalsa College in Amritsar.

Mummy said that when Nanaji died it was as if the whole city lamented. People cried that their protector had died. His body was taken in a chair to the cremation ground so that people could ceremonially view him for the last time.

Nanaji's father, Kishen Singh, had died when his two boys were young. Nanaji's mother – Mummy did not know her name – ground wheat with a hand mill to feed her two boys. They were so poor that when molasses came from a wedding house, the boys would eat it all. They also had more than their share of the bread, for they were always hungry. Nanaji told his granddaughter, "Our mother must have had less then. Nobody told us we were eating our mother's food."

When Nanaji's elder brother was 12 or 14, he opened a stall selling a few things to the English, for they paid more. Afterwards, Nanaji also started a stall selling things. In the process, the boys missed out on getting an education, but they could sign their names. They were not unusual in their time, for only 27 of 100 males in Rawalpindi in 1911 could write and read a letter. Slowly they began doing contract work. Money came into the house. The boys named a village Kishengarh after their father. Their mother saw so much comfort and money that she would sit at home wearing *gokhrai*, heavy gold bracelets. These bracelets told the world that her sons were earning well, that they were filial and looked after their mother.

'And she also died'

Nanaji's house was a house with four uncles, four aunts and numerous cousins, a world ordered by kinship. Nanaji's first wife had died leaving two sons. When I figured out that some of the uncles Mummy often spoke of were her step-uncles rather than "real" uncles, she corrected me, saying they did not think in terms of "real, *sheal*". The blended family was the norm when women died young and men married again. From his second marriage to my mother's grandmother, Nanaji had four daughters and two sons.

When Mummy tells the story of the women of the house, the constant refrain is "And she also died". Sant Kaur, Mummy's mother, was the eldest child from Nanaji's second marriage to Naniji. She was the first daughter in the house. She was married at 13 and died at 21, supposedly of TB. Her husband, Ganga Singh, Mummy's father, had been married before, but his first wife had also died of TB. His in-laws, that is Mummy's Nanaji and Naniji, thought he was a noble man. He came from a modest family, but he was seen as a good match for he had an FA, a degree which signified two years of study after matriculation. Another year of study would complete a BA. He must have been a find, for in 1911 only 348 persons had passed their FA in the whole of Punjab. Moreover, he was a government servant, an inspector with the Post Office, an institution set up by the British in 1854. It was seen as a respectable and well-paid job, with a salary of Rs 30, 35 a month. A carpenter in 1907, for instance, earned Rs 8 a month. In 1911, for one rupee you could buy nearly 14 seers of wheat.

Naniji's second daughter was the Pindi Rani. Nanaji felt that having lost one daughter, this time he would marry his daughter into a princely family. According to family history, she was married to the crown prince of Kapurthala, Jagjit Singh. This story though is not borne out by written history. Mummy's masi was actually married to Jasjit Singh Ahluwalia who was the great grandson of an earlier Rajah of Kapurthala, Nihal Singh who ruled 1837–1852. She also is said to have died of TB leaving behind a son. I had heard her story before. When she went to her husband's home, his mother and aunt and sisters, jealous of the beautiful bride, told the groom that his wife was fat and ugly. The men lived in a different part of the palace from the women. The prince was very young and did not go to see his wife. Mummy says:

Masi was very sad. It wasn't because her husband did not come and see her. She was sad for she felt she was imprisoned. The food would come in gold and silver dishes. She would eat two *phulkas* [unleavened bread so thin that it puffs up] and they would say, "You will get fat". Sit in the sun and they would say "You will get dark". She was a very free spirit and it was as if she was caged. Then her father-in-law heard that the son did not go to the wife. He asked why. When the husband went to his wife, he found her beautiful. She had a child, but two years afterwards she developed TB and died in Simla. I remember Nanaji would bring the son home. But less. I was the one who stayed with him.

The Kapurthala dynasty was a noted one, known for the leadership of Sardar Jassa Singh Ahluwalia, 1718–1783. He was one of the foremost Sikh chiefs, known for his military skill as well as his saintliness. His descendants were supportive of the British and reaped rewards in the shape of titles, royal gun salutes and remission of taxes. They were on the side of the British in 1857 in the pacification of the princely states and in the First World War. As our family belongs to the Ahluwalia *misal* – one of the 12 territorial Sikh groups that emerged in the 18th century – I read the history with particular interest. It became clear how our group could be both ritually low, as by caste we were Kalals, that is, distillers, while at the same time being the leading *misal* due to military power and wealth.

The story goes that Jassa Singh's great-great-grandfather Sadawa (or Sadhu Singh) came from a village near Lahore, which was called

Ahlu, hence the name Ahluwalia. The Kalal connection has its roots in a love story. Sadawa fell in love with a Kalal girl. Sadawa's family objected but later agreed to the marriage as one of the lovers fell dangerously ill. The girl's side agreed but on the condition that Sadawa's children would be married among the Kalals. Hence, Jassa Singh was also called Jassa Kalal and his dynasty Ahluwalia Kalal.

Moving back to Mummy's story, her grandfather's third daughter died unwed, also of TB. It was the youngest daughter, Jasram, to whom Mummy felt close for the rest of her life. This was Darshan's mother, Mummy explains, for Darshan has always been an important part of our lives. Mummy was seven when her aunt Jasram got married at 16 or so.

There was a playfulness about her relationship with this aunt, even though Mummy knew her aunt was older and responsible for her. She laughs, remembering the closeness. When her aunt was getting married, a lot of jewellery was being made for her. So my mother thought she would now get the old pair of beautiful earings with green stones inlaid.

> I said, "Mam Masi, you will give me these earings, won't you?" I thought, I am going to remain here, she is going away. I remember she said, "No". She must have liked them herself. In the evening, Nanaji came and I complained. He laughed at our childishness. He said, "Don't worry. She will give the earings only to you." I don't remember whether she gave them to me or not.

Nanaji felt that the educated, but relatively poor, son-in-law had not made for happiness. Nor had he had a happy experience with the Rajah's house. So for his youngest daughter, Jasram, Nanaji chose a rich man. Mummy said he turned out to be a womaniser and a gambler. Masi Jasram was the unhappiest of all and died many years later in a mental asylum in India.

My mother's father was an important but fringe figure in the early years of her childhood. Growing up in Nanaji's house, Mummy knew that her father's name was Ganga Singh. Sometimes he would come and visit her in Nanaji's house. She had not visited her father's kin, but her father's father used to come and see her. Though she got most of her love from her maternal kin, she said she always knew that in the paternalistic and patriarchal society of Punjab, her father's side was more her own.

Mummy's father married again when she was five. Nanaji had arranged for her father to marry again, so that she would have a home and brothers and sisters to support her. Nanaji was looking ahead to a time when his granddaughter would get married. Then her natal kin, her *paikai,* would be a loving reference point against which she could be a dutiful wife and daughter-in-law.

Every two or three months, Mummy was sent to her father's house for 10 to 15 days. Her father was posted to Jammu. He had a big house over the post office. Her bed used to be placed far from her father and stepmother's bed but in the same room. The treat was that in the morning her father's orderly would buy her sweet fried bread.

Her father was later transferred to Pindi. As the post office house was far away, Nanaji gave Mummy's father and mother a house to live in, rent free. When Mummy was six years old, her brother Khojinder was born.

The last time Mummy saw Nanaji, he was ill. He was lying on a bed in the Post Office Building in Pindi. It was called that because the British had at one time rented it as a post office.

He called me. He called me and held my hand. Even now I remember his words: "*Hai.* See. I used to say, I'd get her married while she was young. I wanted to see her hands with *chura* [the ritual red bangles worn by a new bride] on them. I wanted to see her hands with *chura.* I wanted to see her married." With great anguish he said this.

I did not understand that he would die. But I knew he was in pain and I was very sad. He looked very ill, very weak. "What has happened to him?" I thought.

She was taken to her father's house. At about 10 p.m. they got a message that Sardarji had died.

I cried and cried, cried and cried. I cried a lot. I did not know how I could live without Lallaji [also her name for grandfather]. That much of a shock I could not bear. Three meal times I did not eat.

Her voice chokes. "People would beg me to eat. In the end I ate. I was only a child, nine years old. That was the first shock of my life. It was such a big shock that even now I cannot bear it. Nobody could take his place."

After her grandfather's death, she says, "My life became a bit difficult". She went to live in her father's house, though longing to be with her maternal kin. Her uncles would come and take her back and her grandmother would feed her rich sweetmeats full of nuts, trying to build up her strength. But Mummy's world had been shaken. She was in her father's house, while wanting to be in her grandfather's house. She did not consider her father's house her own.

"Bauji", she says, referring to her father, "had full domain over me." He ensured that her coming and going to her grandfather's house decreased. "He was wise", she says. "There were young boys in the house. And there used to be a lot of servants. I was nine years old." But with her grandfather's death, she says, "I fell into the hands of this mother."

Chapter 3

The girls ate last

———

For a long time it was a secret that my uncles Swaran and Khojinder were actually my mother's step-brothers. Of Baiji, her stepmother, I knew nearly nothing until my mother began to tell her story. I did not know her for she died in 1940, four years before I was born. I had never seen her photograph. I did not know her name. That in itself does not say much. I did not know Mummy's mother's name was Sant Kaur or that Mummy's father's name was Ganga Singh till I began writing the story. I never heard my mother tell the name of her Naniji. But as it turned out, Baiji's name was also Sant Kaur. It was a strange coincidence that Mummy's father had married three women, all of whom were called Sant Kaur.

From honoured guest to stepdaughter

When Nanaji died and Mummy went to live with her father and stepmother, her status changed from that of honoured guest to step-daughter. There were two major areas of conflict. The first was over food, an area where Baiji ruled. It was also the arena where the differences between men and women, boys and girls, were most evident. The second tussle was over jewellery. Baiji sought possession of the previous wife's jewellery as a symbolic expression of her status.

Talking of the first two years in her father's house with her step-mother, Mummy lowers her voice. They were hard years, she says, and then suggests that perhaps this is not something I want to write about. Baiji would serve Bauji in the largest plate, then Khojinder, her brother, who was born when she was six. "Baiji herself would have little", Mummy says, "but mine was always the smallest. I knew which portion was mine, because she gave me the least."

The contrast with her grandfather's house was stark. My mother laughs painfully. Baiji herself would have no breakfast. She would drink tea and give tea to Mummy too. No milk and no breakfast.

Later, when Mummy visited Baiji's village, she found it was the general practice that the girls ate after the boys and ate less. Mummy said Baiji's behaviour then became clear:

> Even if she had had her own daughter, she would have given her less. But I used to get very angry. I used to think she gives me less because she is my stepmother. She did not stint on food as such. I could have as much *roti* as I wanted. But on summer mornings she would not give me breakfast. Don't know why. Just like that. Even now it pains me to remember that every third morning she would give me a drink of milk diluted with water only. She would give me nothing to eat in the morning.

Winters were different, for Bauji went to work at 9 a.m. and Mummy and Khojinder also went to school at the same time. Swaran was ten years younger than Mummy and was still at home. A favourite meal was *roti*, that is bread cooked on a griddle, with cauliflower in the morning. Baiji would put *ghee* inside – to get the *roti* a bit crisp – then crumple it till the air came out. It was so delicious that after Baiji's death, Mama Swaran used to ask Mummy to make him a *roti* with cauliflower like Baiji used to make. But in summer when she left for school at 7 a.m., those were the mornings without food.

"I used to get four paise as a scholarship every morning", Mummy said. This was a time when four paise made an anna and 16 annas made a rupee.

> Baiji would give me two paise out of it, and with that I could get a *puri*. She would think, "What does she need to eat here? She can eat a *puri*." So then during the break, at 9 or 10, I would eat a *puri*. I began to take the money too. She would keep the money under a cloth near the fire. I was hungry. She found out, and I told her, "Yes, I have taken the money." She got angry. But she could not string me up, could she? So I got into the habit of stealing. I would eat two *puris* then.

Bauji knew that Baiji did not give his daughter breakfast. He would get angry with Baiji and tell her to give the girl a glass of milk to drink. There would be a fight, but Mummy says that for all that anger and fighting, Bauji too did not ensure that she was well fed.

The difference between girls and boys was clear whenever it came to food. When almonds came from Kashmir, Khojinder had pockets full of them, as he used to stammer. Afterwards, she would bully Khojinder and get some almonds from him. If corn came from the land, the biggest corn cob went to Khojinder. Mummy says she remembers that when she was ten, she raised a ruckus that she wanted the bigger corn cob. Bauji got angry with Baiji and they started fighting. Mummy says, "When they started fighting I forgot the corn."

Mummy says she tried not to show her resentment or complain about her mother, for it would lead to fights. But that meant she was never good at directly asking for what she wanted.

She became weak and began to have bouts of fever. Bauji began to fear his daughter would get TB like her mother. But then, a Muslim tenant on their land in Dehra Khalsa, who could not pay his rent, gave them his buffalo. That was the saving of her.

I could then drink as much buttermilk as I liked. Baiji would not stop me. Even in the coldest months, in December and January, I would drink three to four glasses of buttermilk. She would give me milk sometimes, but watery.

The return of the jewellery

My mother was 11 before she understood why Baiji was so harsh with her. As the wife of a widower, she felt she had a right to the previous wife's jewellery. However, this jewellery was with Naniji, who was keeping it safe for her granddaughter. Wanting the jewellery, Baiji would curse Mummy's mother. She kept saying her rights had been trampled upon, that because of this stepdaughter, she did not have the jewellery.

When Mummy understood, she persuaded Naniji to hand over

the jewellery. Both Naniji and her aunt Jasram remonstrated that
the jewellery was her mother's and so should be hers. But Mummy
convinced them that her life in her father's house was not worth
living if Baiji did not get the jewellery. It was 50 to 60 tolas (500 to
600 g) worth of jewellery, a lot even for those times. Baiji did not
keep much of it. Some got sold when Bauji and Baiji built their own
house. And some of it she gave to Mummy at her marriage.

After Baiji received the jewellery, Mummy says:

> She was nice to me. I was given full importance in putting away
> things, cooking, serving food. All the keys were with me. The
> money. Everything. I was in charge of the house. When I fought
> with my brothers, she would not take their side. There was a lot
> of love in the house. I don't remember her doing anything to give
> me sorrow then.

Despite improved relations, there continued to be a difference
between girls and boys when it came to eating and drinking. "That
was the tradition at the time", Mummy says.

> In the morning, I would make *paranthas* for Khojinder and
> Swaran, But not for me. I couldn't make one for myself. It was
> her rule. Sometimes I would make a bigger *parantha* so that there
> would be some left over for me to eat. Baiji herself did not eat. She
> would heap it on the boys.

Mummy remembered this difference and it coloured her memories of
life in her father's house. Had she ever talked of it with her brothers?
She said she had tried with Khojinder once, but he did not want to
hear anything that might be seen as critical of his mother. The difference between girls and boys in the food they ate was so ingrained
in society as to be nearly invisible. Her greatest pain was, however,
reserved for her father. She says:

> I loved my father. But I wondered why he didn't force her to give

me good food. My father was a very stern man. The whole house cowered under him. He was very honest. A very good son. A very good brother. A very good man. But some things men don't want to know. Some things are beyond telling.

To give Baiji her due, Mummy said Baiji did not tell her sons, Khojinder and Swaran, that she was their stepsister until they were quite grown. Khojinder says:

We came to know years after our birth that there was a step relationship. It dawned on me that there were two sets of maternal grandmothers, two sets of mother's brothers. Then Baiji explained. But it was such a nice part of my mother, we never found any difference.

Once a woman of the clan asked me, "Does your sister love you like a real sister?" I told her, "I have one sister. She loves me. I love her. She is my sister."

Mummy's stepmother Baiji, Sant Kaur, renamed 'Gurbachan Kaur'

Swaran too had to find out for himself after his sister was married. He was seven years old and wondered why his sister had a different set of relatives. He was also trying to figure out his father's story and asked his brother, "How come Father had two marriages before and how come he had no children?" Swaran remembers, "Brother said, 'Stupid! Don't you know? Bhaini [Sister]'. Mother was heaping curses on Brother, and saying, 'Don't say that, don't say that'."

Mummy says that in the long run Baiji was a good stepmother. It was a difficult role.

> When my Nanaji was alive, I was so spoilt by his love that no matter who my mother might have been, I would not have been able to manage with her. After he died, my security ended. Slowly, slowly, over two years, I adjusted. I accepted that this is my house. This is where I have to stay. But it was very difficult. I realised how much I had missed when I had my own children. It is hard for a child to be without a father, but without a mother, a child is finished.

Baiji herself had little choice in the way her own life turned out. She had had five years of schooling. Even that amount of schooling was unusual, for in 1911, only 9 of every 100 women in Rawalpindi were literate. She was 16 or 17 when she was engaged to Bauji. The match was proposed by her cousin, who had married into Nanaji's family. Mummy says:

> Baiji did not even know she was engaged for the engagement was settled in Lahore while she was in Amritsar. She had a dream that the two sisters – my mother and her younger sister who had also died – were sitting and my mother had turned her face away in anger. The younger sister asked, "Why is your face all burnt up? Sant [Baiji] has come and you don't talk to her." Then in the dream, my mother tells her sister, "Don't you know? She is coming in my place." Baiji woke up. When she went back to Lahore where she lived, she discovered she was engaged.

She was married to a stern man 26 years her senior, who had already been married twice before and had a child. On her marriage, Baiji's name was changed from Sant Kaur to Gurbachan Kaur. Changing a girl's personal name at marriage was not unusual in Punjabi patrilineal society. But in her case, it was also hoped that the change would ward off the fate of the first two wives who had died of TB.

Her world was "to serve Bauji and to be a good wife", Mummy says. "She did not see much happiness." She died in Lahore of a tumour when she was 42. Bauji outlived his third wife by seven years and died at 75.

Chapter 4

Married in Rawalpindi

———

In 8th class, my mother came first in the Rawalpindi district. She won a scholarship for the senior school for girls which had just opened in Pindi. But Bauji said she was 13 and had to stop going to school. Baiji was also not happy with Mummy continuing. Teachers from the school came to try to persuade them to send their daughter to school but, like most other parents of girls in Pindi, they stood their ground. The girl is "grown-up", they said.

The engagement

At 16, Mummy was engaged. A different note comes into my mother's voice when she talks of Baiji after her engagement and marriage. She begins to talk of her naturally as her mother, as Manji.

Bauji had been to a wedding in Sialkot, where he visited the house of a postmaster, who was from the Pindi kinship group, the *Baradari*. Bauji was much taken by the face and bearing of the eldest son, Pargat Singh. Their living style was good. It did not matter that the boy was 13 years older than his daughter. The most important thing was that the boy was a doctor. He thought that getting his daughter married to a doctor would save her from TB. He had lost two wives to TB and was afraid that his daughter was weak and would be dead before she was 36 or 37.

Bauji's sister was against the match for she had heard that the boy had been "ill" and that he had a bad temper. But Bauji countered, "He is a doctor. He is a doctor." More talk surfaced. A cousin told Mummy that the man was mad. When Baiji told Bauji what the cousin had said, he said the girl was herself infatuated with Pargat Singh, my father. Moreover this cousin had been proposed to him but their suit was rejected because they had a lot of TB in their family. So they discounted this talk of "illness", saying the rumour was an exaggeration of stress during his pre-medical examinations before beginning his medical course.

Few knew the whole story but at the engagement my father fought with Baiji, his future mother-in-law. Baiji was also upset because he was paying untoward attention to the cousin who had earlier told them he was mad. Seeing her mother disturbed, Mummy also felt hurt. "He was 'up' then", Mummy said. "We of course did not know anything of 'up' and 'down.'"

When more talk began to surface about the boy, Bauji wanted to break the engagement. There had been a mistake. But there were no other proposals in sight. It was a matter of caste. There were few educated boys of the Bhagra caste or castes of equal status. Bauji also worried that boys would be scared away because his daughter's mother had died of TB.

Mama Swaran says another disadvantage was that Mummy had buckteeth. It was only after her marriage that she fell in the bathroom and the dentist made her two new front teeth. Bauji was also more worried because Mummy was actually 18, rather than 16, when she was engaged. Bauji had lessened her age by two years so that she would be more marriageable. This was a reaction to the fact that he had added three years to his age when he was looking for a job. But that meant he had to retire three years earlier. So with his children, he made them out to be younger than they were.

Bauji and Baiji considered the engagement one way then another. Sometimes Bauji would falter. At other times Baiji would think it was a mistake. Mama Khojinder remembers these discussions. He says:

My mother was against it. My mother cried a number of times, "Look, I will be blamed if she has difficulty." They had heard he was not well. Moreover, there was a lot of age difference. My mother used to tell Bauji, "She is a good girl. We will find a man."

Baiji, however, could not insist. She was afraid that people would say the stepmother stood in the way of the girl marrying a doctor. Mummy says, "I also helped her by saying, Never mind. Wherever I have been engaged, let it be.'"

The marriage date was fixed. Mummy was happy she was getting married. Khojinder would tease Mummy, shouting, "P A R G A T, P A R G A T", spelling out her fiancé's name. She of course never called him by name. Mummy had seen his photograph. She had no other contact with her fiancé. Whenever he came to the house, she was supposed to disappear from sight. So total was the avoidance that once when my father came unexpectedly and found my mother swinging on the verandah, her feet touching the roof, she jumped straight off to go and hide herself.

It was a happy time. Her cousins made up a play called "O Beloved". My mother says:

> I thought I would go away to another house, and maybe it will be a better house than this. I will be well treated. I will wear beautiful clothes. I will sit in a palanquin, with one man in the front and one man at the back.

The preparations for the wedding were exciting. There was a lot of music. Relatives came to stay. Clothes and jewellery came from Mummy's parents and kin and from the groom's side. There were a lot of clothes, maybe 25 to 30 sets.

> For my wedding, Baiji gave me my mother's heavy pendant. Baiji gave the bangles that Nanaji had given me to my grandmother-in-law, your father's Dadijee. Baiji made me a set of gold jewellery and nice clothes. From the house they gave me 10–15 tolas (100–150 g). My mother's kin put in 30–35 tolas (300–350 g). Some I got from my in-laws. Well, it was a good trousseau.

She was taken to the roof to see the groom arriving on a mare. There was no custom of *jai mala* in her days, where the bride and groom garland each other. Of the actual wedding, she says nothing. After she got married, Mummy sat in the palanquin to songs of farewell to go to her marital home 20 minutes away. My father had wanted to go in a car but Bauji was against the groom and bride sitting together.

So halfway to her new home, my father asked his wife to get down from the palanquin.

They had a band at the front, the empty palanquin following, and the husband and wife in all their marriage finery, walking together, bringing up the rear. People on the street laughed at this unusual sight. My father said his only regret was he had not dismissed the band and the palanquin. And so my mother started her married life before she was 17. Or 19.

Aijee Pitajee together

"I couldn't say that after my marriage I was unhappy", Mummy says. "People did not look for happiness. There should be food to eat, clothes to wear, a house to live in. It is all right."

She did not know what to expect, even though a recently married friend had tried to tell her. She said:

Five to seven days passed. Nothing happened. He'd take my clothes off and not do very much. But I didn't know what was to be done. My mother's sister-in-law would ask, "What has happened? What has happened?" I in turn asked, "What was supposed to happen?"

He slept with me 10 or 12 days after the wedding. About two years later, Lata was born. Four years after that, Ranjana was born. I wasn't very unhappy or anything. I had my house. I had my children. My naniji used to love me very much. It was all right. I was quite satisfied. I wasn't used to sex, nor did I have any expectation. I was very happy.

Pitajee had taken Mummy to his ancestral home in Rawalpindi, on Rai Sahib Narain Das Street, in the old part of the town near Saidpuri Gate. This was where they lived from 1928 to the early 1940s. They had the house to themselves, for Pitajee's father and siblings continued to live in Sialkot.

It was a single-storey house. Houses were built close to each other across a street 6–8 feet wide. You could call out and talk to your neighbours from one house to another. An open gutter ran along the street. At one end of the street there was a small mosque and you could hear the call to prayer five times a day.

My sisters remember their house as being full of activity. There were kinfolk at home and other kin regularly visited. There was the singing of folk songs at marriages, hymns at religious gatherings. Money was scarce but life seemed full. My mother cooked well, sang well, sewed well. She obeyed her husband and looked after his elders with care. She accepted his domination and temper, and saw herself as content. In Rawalpindi, Lata and Ranjan remember there was a lot of laughter. "Even Pitajee?" I ask. "Yes, yes, everybody used to laugh."

For Lata and Ranjan, who are 15 and 11 years older than I, Rawalpindi was the reference point for family life. Ranjan remembers her life in Rawalpindi, the details clearly etched. The house was built in the Moorish style. From the street, one had to climb a few steps to a landing, 6 by 8 feet, as in New York brownstones. The door was above the landing. This door used to remain open most of the time, screened with a bamboo blind. It was the pre-entry area of the house. In the afternoons, Pitajee used to have his bed there so that he could catch any breeze that passed by. On one side was a small room reserved for receiving male visitors.

There was another door through which you entered the brick-paved inner courtyard. This spacious courtyard was the most memorable feature of the house, with plants and vines with bluebells. When my mother built our house in Delhi, she replicated the landing and the inner courtyard.

My uncle Swaran remembers that to one side of the inner courtyard there was a dressing room. It was there that Pitajee delivered Lata and Ranjan. The two large rooms were as large as a big modern apartment, Ranjan says. Each room had a store room behind. There were also some small rooms. Mummy and Pitajee would sleep in one of the large rooms, and Pitajee's father's mother – Dadiji – stayed in the other bedroom. Lata and Ranjan would sleep in either of these rooms. Guests came and fitted themselves in wherever they chose. In the summer, everybody slept on the roof.

The store room behind Mummy and Pitajee's room was particularly special. As children, Lata and Ranjan would go there and throw spent bulbs through the window. The bulbs would explode like crackers as they hit the wall of the next house.

There was an old style kitchen. Most of the time they had a cook. Ranjan says:

> The best part was that before going to school, we used to have our regular lunch meal at about 8 or 9 in the morning. We sat on the floor on colourful round cane seats with a cane stand on which the *thalis* [steel-rimmed plates] would be placed. It was a very nice cosy feeling to eat the *chapatis* just as they were made. I used to like cauliflower very much, because it was partly raw, as the cook didn't have time to cook it enough.

There were other routines to the day. Lata says, "From 2 p.m. to 4 p.m., Aijee [Lata and Ranjan called Mummy Aijee] and Pitajee would sleep. Ranjan and I used to come in quietly and have our food. We thought of them as together: Pitajee Aijee are doing this. Towards the end you never thought of them as together."

Every evening after dinner, Mummy, Pitajee, Lata and Ranjan would go for a walk. They would walk past Bauji's place, past Mai Viro di Banni and then go up to the Rai Bahadur Buta Singh Saraan, a mile and a half away. They would often also stop at Masi Darshan's house. Ranjan says:

> It's like another lifetime. There were hardly any cars on the road. People used to sleep on the side of the road. One day, I was sleepy and looking down, I saw a snake, a big straw-coloured snake on the road. We could hardly wait to get home to tell Bauji. It was such important news. I told him we almost died.

Bauji immediately announced, "On Sunday we will have *purai*." This was the big treat. There was a shack in one corner near the house, a few minutes away, where Buddhu – this couldn't have been his real name, for it means "stupid" – would make chickpeas that were called

Buddhu's chickpeas. On Sundays, he would make *purai*, fermented dough with sugar and honey. You could buy them and take them home. Whenever any important event needed to be marked, Bauji would announce, "Next Sunday we will have *purai*."

Closeness of kin

It was the closeness of family, living next to each other, that Lata and Ranjan remember most vividly of the period between 1929 and 1940. Lata and Ranjan would be sent on Saturday afternoon to their maternal grandparents' house for the weekend. Baiji would wash their hair. Lata saw her grandparents' house as her own house. She says:

> Bauji was very different with us than with his own children. He used to feed us. He taught Ranjana [Ranjan] how to wear a shirt. I always thought that home was mine. I got so much love there. I used to go to Aijee's house for four days just to study.
>
> Baiji used to give me a lot of affection. If she did not give it to her daughter, she made up with me. Ranjan used to stay more at home. Baiji died after she developed a tumour. After that also I used to stay at Bauji's place with Swaran Mama and Khojinder Mama.

For Ranjan, the big attraction was to go and play with Jimmy, the German Shepherd, in Baiji's house. Ranjan also went to the grandparents' house for all the things she got. She says:

> I would ask every weekend, "Baiji, next week what will you give me?" She would give me a colourful *dupatta* or she would make me something. I made it a condition that whenever I come, there will be a gift. Lata never asked for anything. She got the gift also but I was the one who did the asking.
>
> I would ask for colourful rice – green and yellow and red. Then Mamaji would show me a rice grain with yellow and red and green on it. He would tell me, "See how Baiji has coloured every grain of rice for you." And I would believe him.

Pitajee's paternal grandmother, Dadiji, lived with them till she died. Ranjan says they used to call her Baiji also. She used to want to get her back scratched.

I must have been five. And I would sit there and scratch her back. And she would say, "Hai, it's on fire." I'd be frightened. I would ask, "Baiji, you are on fire? Where is the fire?" Everybody would be listening. She would say scratching was burning her and wanted me to scratch a little more.

She is the Dadiji who embroidered the *bagh* that I now have. It is very finely embroidered in gold coloured silken thread that Dadiji's son, my grandfather, had brought from Shanghai where he was posted as a postmaster. It was the custom to drape your daughter-in-law in a *bagh* at the wedding. Dadiji had embroidered it perhaps a hundred years ago for the bride of her second grandson, Pitajee's younger brother Appar. My uncle Appar never got married. As Dadiji had entrusted it to Mummy's care and it was one of the heirlooms Mummy had brought with her at Partition, Mummy formally asked my father's permission before draping it on me at my wedding. The embroidery is so fine that one can hardly see the maroon cotton below. Later, it became the centrepiece of the exhibition Textiles and Tales: Punjabi Women in Victoria that I initiated at the Immigration Museum in Melbourne. As the curator and I were examining the condition of the exhibits for insurance purposes, on one edge I found Appar's name written in Gurmukhi in black ink.

My father's grandmother was given a small pill of opium every day. She died at 87. But towards the end, she was in a coma. The neighbours kept a close watch on her condition. Lata says there was a woman in the next house, whom they called "Bhuajee" (father's sister), even though she was not related, who every six hours would shout:

"Lata, is everything all right?" I would say, "Bhuajee, yes things are fine." Next time she checked, "Lata. Is everything fine?", I said,

"No, it is not." "Oh, terrible, terrible. Why are you making *phulkas*? Now, it is I who will send you the food."

The neighbour was upset Mummy was breaking the code of not cooking in a house where a person had recently died. But Mummy came out and said, "The grandson says he is very hungry, that he does not believe in all these customs. Bhuajee, now he has had his food. You can send us food in the morning."

Mummy at Mama Khojinder's wedding

Pitajee decided to wait for all the relatives to arrive before they cremated his grandmother. This too was extraordinary, for usually the body is cremated the same day or the next. Pitajee kept the body for two nights. It was summer. Everybody was having a hilarious time, with the body on the other side. They started joking with Pitajee, "Now that you have put the body on ice for two days, why don't you put the body in the sun for two days?" Ranjan remembers that Aijee's family brought a lot of food. Huge baskets of cashew nuts and pistachios. She says, "They were very rich."

Ranjan, who was about five or six at the time, was in the next room with a fever and was crying because nobody was paying any attention to her. She remembers somebody saying to her, "Why are you crying? She had to go. She was already old. Why are you crying?"

It was an open house with kin coming in and out, often staying for a while. Pitajee's eldest sister's children would come and stay for the summer. His younger sister Tripat came to stay with her family. Once a week, Masi Darshan and her brother Bhajan would come for lunch. Mama Swaran would come with his dog Jimmy. Mama Khojinder came to stay for a stretch when he was in college.

For a time, one of Pitajee's aunts – his father's elder brother's wife – also stayed in their house. Ranjan says:

> People were mistreating her where she was staying. She had some kind of obsessive compulsive disorder – of course we didn't know the term at that time. She was constantly washing her hands. She would take some ash and wash her hands. Then she would wash her hands again. It was fascinating for young people. She stayed for a few months.

My mother said her house was renowned as the house where old people were well looked after. The neighbours would joke that if you have any old woman you do not want, just send her to Inder's house.

Pitajee "falls ill"

The even rhythm of life in Rawalpindi was broken by my father's episodes of manic-depressive psychosis. Though Mummy's family also had its share of mental illness – at least one uncle and one aunt were afflicted – few people at the time knew about manic-depressive psychosis. In my family, it was always said that my father "fell ill". Early in her marriage, her father-in-law took Mummy aside and told her that his son was sometimes extravagant and sometimes lethargic. He told her not to get worried but to make sure that she looked after the house and money herself. That is why he said they had not hosted a wedding dinner from their side. He said, "You can eat for six months on that money."

Mummy did not understand, for she had only seen my father when he was "up" during the engagement and wedding. When the relatives left after the wedding, he became lethargic. My mother thought that this was the way it would be. He would remain in bed until 4 p.m. and sometimes not even get up to eat. In the beginning, she would tell him to get up, bathe, have his food. Later, she says, she became used to it. If he wanted to lie down, she would let him lie down.

She told her mother that he didn't get up in the morning. Her mother said, "Yes, Bauji is worried. People are saying Doctor Sahib is so engrossed in sex that he doesn't get out of the house. So Bauji suggests that maybe we should take you home, or the boy will get weak." Mummy said:

> I told her it was nothing like that. When he is lethargic, there is no possibility of that. Manji told Bauji. He was so upset, saying, "I have put a knife to my daughter's throat." My mother said he could not sleep at night. Then I talked to my mother because I was shy of speaking with my father. I said if you had had me married to a perfectly normal man and he became mad, would you have turned away from the marriage? It is all written. I am not upset. I comforted her. I really was not upset. I had become used to it. I told myself it was not his fault that he did not have good health, that he did not have money. He is faithful. He is honest. I am happy with my children. When he is down, at least he does not make noise, does not get angry.

Normally he was a domineering husband, accustomed to having the house and family run the way he wanted. When he became manic, his bad temper escalated to abuse and violence. Mama Khojinder remembers the many days Pitajee was violent. He says:

> He would sometimes come to our house in the middle of the night. There would be a knock, and he would say, "I have come.

I am going to sleep here." We would put a bed there. He would be accompanied by two servants.

It was a very sad thing. What could anybody do? Even the neighbours used to see it. My mother had a very difficult role. She would get up at 2 a.m., 3 a.m. to attend to him. Sometimes he would abuse her. Bauji, my father, used to watch it. Once or twice he wept.

Despite this violence and madness, the doctor part of Pitajee remained sane during his manic episodes. Mama Khojinder remembers that, once or twice, a cousin came to consult him. "Bhaiajee [sister's husband] wrote a prescription and it was right, though he was completely off." He even gave a prescription for a second medicine in case the first did not work. When the cousin had the prescriptions checked, they were the most appropriate medicines that could have been given.

Nevertheless, the manic depressive psychosis meant that my father was not able to earn much money for most of his life. He had opened a clinic in Rawalpindi shortly before his marriage. When he was "up", he was short-tempered and tactless and so lost patients. When he was "down", he would not go to the clinic at all. He had been a brilliant student in Lahore, winning gold medals in women's diseases and mental health. The few patients he had, stayed with him.

Whatever money there was, Mummy controlled. This situation continued even when my father had money for six years when he was with the Army (1941–1946). The family was somewhat protected against the lack of money. They were living in my father's ancestral house, so there was no rent to be paid. There was money enough for Mummy to frequently hop on the train to Amritsar to visit her aunt, Baiji's sister. While Naniji was alive, she did not let them feel the shortage of money. Naniji would open her stores so they could take bales of silk and velvet for clothes; as a result, the family was the best dressed in the neighbourhood. I still have at home a mirror with bone inlay that was part of a dressing table Naniji bought for them when the family went to stay with her during the summers in the

Murree Hills.

Moreover, Nanaji had left a will providing Mummy Rs 25 a month for life. With that Rs 25, they could buy a whole month's ration in the 1930s. The postman would come with that Rs 25 money order even in the 1960s. Mummy also received Rs 4000 as a lump sum from her Nanaji. He had intended the money to pay for her education as a doctor. This was a leap of faith in his time, for in 1899, of the 208 students enrolled in the Lahore Medical College, only eight were women. But the money got spent paying for my father's bouts of mental illness. Most of my mother's jewellery was sold for the same reason.

The picture wasn't as comfortable as Mummy or Ranjan painted it. Lata remembers a time when she had only one faded *dupatta* (the veil that goes with the traditional Punjabi dress) and Mummy had only one *dupatta*. She says:

> Aijee was ill and had a terrible earache. She was screaming and Pitajee had called another doctor. When I was going to school, I saw Aijee's *dupatta* in the cupboard. I thought, today my mother is not going anywhere, and wore her *dupatta*.
>
> The doctor who came said the pain is very severe; we have to take her to such and such a place. Pitajee looked for the *dupatta* and there was no *dupatta*. Aijee said, "This is Lata's *dupatta*. She must have taken mine."
>
> Pitajee had no sensitivity. He came to school with my *dupatta* in his hand and tore Aijee's *dupatta* away. I still remember the children's faces, I remember my father and the way he did it, the way the children laughed after he left.

This incident stands out because they seldom spoke about feeling poor, though money was scarce. Ranjan says:

> Foodwise, we were never short. Only later, I found out that it was "borrowed" stuff. Before Independence, they were satisfied living in Rawalpindi and getting all their provisions on credit. There was no money in the house. But nobody would refuse a doctor.

I never felt that we were poor. Pitajee and Aijee kept that fact from us. Whatever we asked for, we got. When we would go to Pitajee's clinic and say we wanted to eat fish, Pitajee would dole out the money. Sometimes it was the only money he had made that day. During our childhood in Rawalpindi, we never got a "No" and we never heard "We can't afford it". So Pitajee and Aijee were on the same wavelength at that period.

Whereas with you [after Partition], when you would ask for a yo-yo or something, he'd say, "There isn't enough money." Aijee would correct him and say, "Don't give her the wrong idea". And Pitajee would say, "It isn't a wrong idea. I don't have the money." But Aijee was remembering the older philosophy that they would give even if it meant using credit.

Though the family was hard up, they usually had a cook. Nuro, the Muslim midwife, would come to massage Mummy and wash her hair. She helped nurse Mummy when she was ill with typhoid. When my mother spoke of her through the years, her voice would often be tearful. Sometimes it was only Nuro who understood the unspoken pain, the lack of money behind the gracious facade, the joys of the children. Nuro was woven into the texture of their lives and became involved with the rest of Mummy's natal family, so much so that when Mama Khojinder and his wife Mami Mohinder came to stay in our Rawalpindi house between 1942 and 1944, Nuro was there for the birth of their two children.

Years later, when Mummy talked of Pindi, she hoped Nuro had taken over their house. Mama Khojinder thinks that maybe the house keys were with Nuro. Mummy had heard from one of the old family retainers that Nuro's family was in our old house and was very pleased about it. For a while Mummy and I talked of putting an advertisement in the papers to try to find Nuro's family. In 1994 I planned to go to Pindi and look her up, but then the Babri Mosque affair happened in India and it was no time for a Sikh woman to be alone in Pindi. I suspect my mother did not want to probe the past. We let it be.

The Army

In 1941 my father joined up as a doctor in the army. His salary was Rs 300 a month. For the first time in their lives, a regular substantial income came into the house. Every month they would send Rs 125 to Pitajee's sister to repay a loan of some thousands they had taken. He was posted to Karachi, then Iraq and finally to Meerut, where I was born in 1944.

For Mummy, Karachi and Meerut were happy memories. She found Karachi beautiful with beaches and breezes. When Mummy talked of Karachi, she talked of her Sindhi neighbours, and how there was money in the house. Mummy says she thought there was more than enough for the housekeeping so she would get a suit made at the beginning of the month. But they had also hired an expert cook who wanted expensive ingredients for the meals and so the last few days of the month would be difficult. Meerut too was good. There was fruit. A male servant, Prem Singh, was hired to look after me. He got teased a lot because of his role as Nanny, but he remained with us in one way or another in Delhi for the next ten years. Bauji came to stay. Ranjan went to an English medium school. Bhua Tripat and her two children came to stay for the summer holidays. Mama Khojinder must have come too for there is a photograph of Manjit, my cousin, and me playing in the garden of the house. Mummy said:

> In Meerut we enjoyed the outer world. Good company, good money. You were born there. I became busy with you. The house was an old MES bungalow. Three or four bedrooms, drawing room, dining room, kitchen. There was a small garden outside. It was a Lieutenant Colonel's accommodation, though your father was a captain.

Pitajee had the opportunity to specialise in radiology but he was not enthusiastic about it. They were living comfortably. There was an interesting social life. They spent their time eating and drinking. The children played badminton on the lawn. But without the specialisation, he was disbanded from the army after his five-year contract came to an end. This was in 1946.

Family photograph, 1946 in Meerut. Lata, Pitajee, me,
Mummy and Ranjan

They did not want to go back to the life they had lived in Rawalpindi. Mummy said:

By now we had a bit of status. We were used to staying in bungalows. Good company. Rawalpindi was a bit backward. There were relatives and little else. The house was in an alley. All of us had good memories of Karachi. A very clean city with beautiful houses. Sanmukh [Pitajee's youngest brother] had a friend who said he knew people in Karachi and through him we got a very nice house. We thought your Pitajee would open a shop there. And when the shop began to do well, we would settle there.

Partition was already in the air. But my parents decided the family would settle in Karachi. This was in January 1947. They never saw Rawalpindi again.

Chapter 5

Chasing the past

———

I am trying to put myself in the story, and think a visit to Lahore and Rawalpindi would bring alive the context of the first 36 years of my mother's life. I also want to capture the visual texture of her life, for she did not talk in images.

Twice I had planned to go, but it had not been a good time to visit Pakistan. Getting a visa was not a problem, for after my first marriage, I had become a Malaysian citizen. Mama Swaran and Mama Khojinder were opposed to my going. They worried about my safety, my travelling alone, in the aftermath of the Indian Airlines hijacking in January 2000. They were also afraid about my returning to Pakistan, a place from which we had fled. Maybe I would not be able to come back. Rawalpindi was a place to be dreamt about but not to visit. More than 50 years since Partition had not reduced the dread.

Ranjan, in New York, did not tell me not to go but she said more than once that I should watch the situation carefully, read the Pakistani papers on the Internet to anticipate the situation. I too got concerned when I was not able to contact anyone in Pakistan on the phone from India – the circuits were always busy – and so I embarked on the much anticipated trip with no bookings, just three names and telephone numbers.

"Lahore, Lahore, Lahore, Oiee..."

Pashi, Professor Thakur Singh's daughter, came with me by car from Amritsar to Wagah, where I walked across the Indian border, crossed no-man's land and reached Pakistan. The Number 2 bus leaves Wagah for Lahore. I sat with the women in the front section, partitioned from the other half of the bus. With me was a woman from Lahore now resident in Canada, who had just been to Amritsar to look at the ancestral home she had abandoned in 1947. She dissuaded me from taking a taxi to Lahore and so I was on the bus.

We leave India. I expect to feel different. There are buffaloes on the road. There are houses with half-baked bricks, cowdung cakes drying on the unfinished walls. Men drive open carts loaded with fodder. The brass containers which in Amritsar dangle from the milkman's cycle are loaded on top of the fodder. There are minarets in the distance and the writing is in Urdu on a green background.

The bus stops every few moments and the conductor shouts, "Lahore, Lahore, Lahore, Oiee…". Slowly the bus fills up. Women heave themselves up the high steps at the front of the bus. One woman is wearing a magenta *kameez* with gold embroidery. Another wears a red velvet suit with a midnight blue shawl. Yet another wears a yellow suit, a pink pullover, red, white and gold coloured sandals and a black *burka*. Most wear glass bangles and a nose ring.

The conductor comes around from the back of the bus to issue tickets to the women travelling without a male companion. An older woman takes out coins from a Fair and Lovely cold cream bottle. As I look at her, while taking notes, she asks the woman from Canada about me. When they hear I can speak Punjabi, they ask me where I come from, where I am going.

I am not sure whether I am the only woman travelling alone, but I am the only woman in the bus whose head is not covered in one way or another. But apparently what is most distinctive about me is the quality of the hair dye I use. One woman asks me to write down the name, so that her husband can get it from India on his frequent trading trips across the border. The Canadian woman says, "In India, women are convinced the Pakistani dye is better."

Lahore is 28 km from Wagah. We have already been in the bus for more than an hour. The conductor is doing better than he had hoped in filling up the bus. Now he is trying to persuade the children to go with the men at the back. There are women sitting on the gear box, on the floor, on the three bench seats lining the back and the sides of the front section.

"They should make our section bigger", says a naval wife going on to Rawalpindi. She moves up further towards the corner to make room for a highly rouged little girl.

The bus goes slowly, stopping often. As we near Lahore, two women get on wearing shawls drawn across their mouths to double as a kind of half *burka*. Another two get on, their hands freshly hennaed. On the right we pass shops with long canes and bamboo blinds. "See, see", says the Canadian woman, "the Shalimar Gardens", pointing to the walls surrounding them. And soon a pavement full of posters for sale. Then we see the Kinnaird High School for girls on Empress Road. None of my family went there, but Lata went to Kinnaird College. Lahore begins to feel more familiar.

The Canadian woman alerts me that I need to get off. The conductor says, "Cross the road, turn right near the mosque and take the Number 3 bus." I collect my laptop, satchel, handbag and overnight case and suggest to the Canadian woman that perhaps I should take an auto rickshaw. "No, no", she says. "That is too expensive. The bus will only cost you Rs 2." I do not argue for I know it is she who has brought me to this point for Rs 8 instead of the Rs 200 that the taxi driver was wanting.

I get down, slip my red shawl over my head and find a No. 3 bus at the bus stop. As we wait, a man comes around chanting, "*Garam, garam dal. Karari, karari dal. Garam garam dal*", the usual chant of vendors selling roasted *gram* in India. The bus starts. Within ten minutes, the conductor points out my hotel. So here I am in Lahore, with my PC and a bag, walking up the driveway of the historical Falleti's Hotel. The hotel has obviously seen better days, but even then I am possibly the only guest who has arrived by bus. The gentleman at the desk, relishing my Punjabi and hearing that my family is from Pindi, decides to shave the rate by Rs 500.

I am in Lahore, the first person in my immediate family to have made the trip back to Pakistan since 1947. Lahore, Rawalpindi and Karachi have framed the family stories but I have no geographical map in my head. So I am surprised that Lahore is not further away. All these years, when my family spoke of Lahore and its famous Anarkali market in terms that implied it was beyond reach, it was just a short bus ride from Amritsar.

I still have to discover Lahore. But as I sit in the auto rickshaw with wooden sides on my way to see Gurdwara Dehra Sahib in the old city – the Gurdwara that marks the martyrdom of our fifth Guru Arjun Dev – I need to tell myself again that I am in Lahore. It has been a simple trip, with a sense of recognition even though I have never been here before.

Search for my family homes

Lahore is only a transit point for I am headed for Rawalpindi. From Lahore, I ring a senior advocate at the Supreme Court, to whom I have an introduction. He invites me to stay. He is a friend of the Ahluwalia *baradari* and knew my father and my mother's Nanaji. For him the immediate attraction of my visit is that I claim to know how to make Buddhu's chickpeas. With Partition, he is left yearning for these chickpeas and only in Delhi now and again does he get a taste of them. Buddhu generally did not give out his recipe but he told Mummy how to get the special flavour. It is one of the recipes she gave me after I got married. So on my first evening in Rawalpindi, I soak the chickpeas along with cardamom, brown cinnamon, bay leaves and green chillies. The next day my hostess and I boil the chickpeas till they are tender. We have been instructed to wait for my host to come back for lunch, so that I can mix the spices in front of him.

When he sees the way I have cut the ginger, he pronounces that the chickpeas are not made in the authentic Buddhu style. The chickpeas come out the way I always make them – dark brown and moist, flavoured with dried mango. The ginger is plentiful, red rather than brown. And brown fried onions, of course. But for him the chickpeas have failed. Perhaps no one can deliver on his memories, but one of my claims to fame is punctured.

My search for my family homes is also a bitter-sweet affair. Rawalpindi is a city of alleys and houses with large wooden doors. I get a glimpse of the same kind of doors in Tarn Taran. We find Nanaji's house in a narrow street with open gutters that must have smelt the same all those years ago. Two people cannot walk abreast in the street. My uncles remember these streets as having a drain running through the centre. The street is so narrow that a neighbouring house has a covered overpass linking the houses on either side. The houses rise close and high, so close that it is impossible to get a full picture of the house. So when the milkman's buffalo was on the street, all traffic must have had to push the buffalo aside to pass. My host explains that Sikhs built their houses this way to resist invasion.

The house is larger than I imagined from my mother's description. My mother had not talked of the large carved wooden door in the front, perhaps because these doors are found all over the old city. It is a three-storey house built in a quadrangle around an open courtyard.

There is not one roof, but two. The stairs my mother talked of are hemmed in by walls. The stairs leading to the highest roof are narrow and high – only one person at a time can go up or down. And from the roof is a panoramic view of the whole of Rawalpindi and Islamabad. I can also see the hills in the distance and down into the inner courtyard where rooms frame either side.

The owner of the house, who has graciously invited us in, says there are 35 rooms in the house, if you count all of them, large and small. There are no longer factories and offices on the ground floor. The house is occupied by four families, sometimes more. Did I know there was a well? she asks.

We then try to find my mother's marital home. We find the street and the house of Rai Sahib Narain Dass with its beautifully carved balconies. At one end of the street there is the school. It used to be the Khalsa School where my sisters began their schooling, now it is an Islamic school. At the other end is a dainty mosque. My host is 99 per cent sure that it is the pink house with green arches. But this is a two-storey house and my sister had described it as a one-storey house. The owner invites me in, his wife offers me oranges and they show me the house. It is built around an inner courtyard – as are all the Pindi houses I have seen so far – but I can't fit it to my sister's description. Was there a brick courtyard? A bluebell vine growing here? Was there a lime tree? He can't say. The courtyard seems too small for that anyway.

Did Nuro stay here? I ask. But nobody remembers Nuro.

I can't see a house with Moorish architecture, steps leading to a landing, two doors opening from it, another door leading to a brick courtyard. My host says probably it was the house next door, which used to be a one-storey house. Now it is a green house which is two or three storeys high.

I knew the house had no number on it. My aunt said the postman would come around and shout, "Dr Pargat Singh Ji, Dr Pargat Singh Ji", and throw the letters on the porch. My uncle had said it was the fifth house from the end, the second house from the mosque. Everyone in the street indulges me. But now these are shops and there is no one-storey house here, none at least from whose roof Ranjan would have been able to see the snow on the Murree hills.

Another gentleman says, if anyone can remember, it will be the 75-year-old man who lives in the house above. He knows my host. But when I ask him about my father Dr Pargat Singh and about Nuro, he says he has never heard of them. "1947", he says, "so long ago."

I take photographs of the whole street and wonder again at the wisdom of trying to find a house I have never seen. I know I will have to go back and check it again, for I need to take something for my sister to see. Later Ranjan looks at the photographs and says, "Here it is. Here it is. The same steps going up. But I had forgotten we had a room above the porch."

I have better luck with Nanaji's "country home" – Rai Bahadur Buta Singh Saraan – literally an inn of homes linked around a common courtyard. The name remains with the older people. It is on Saidpur Road, but the road is not recognisable from my mother's description. She talked of it as being outside the city on the northern outskirts. But the block of shops that now occupies what used to be Rai Bahadur Buta Singh Saran is still distinct. My host says this residence covered three to four *kanal*, roughly an acre. Till recently, there used to be a large bolted gate, about 12 feet high and 8 feet wide. On both sides of this gate you could see brick houses. The place used to be in the middle of a wilderness with *sheesham* trees around it. Now there are shops at the front, facing a busy road screaming with trucks, cars and scooter rickshaws. It is difficult to imagine an orchard behind the brick buildings.

There was a water tank, Mai Viro di Banni, where the family would go for an evening walk. Nobody knows why it was named so, but the tank was filled in many years ago. In its place is a tonga stand, shops and a stand for gaily coloured Suzuki vans. The place is now called Banni Chowk. The portion of Saidpur Road next to the Chowk is crowded with cars, cycles, rickshaws, with shops selling wedding garlands made of currency, carpets, tents.

I have no luck whatsoever with my grandfather's houses. My mother's father, unlike her grandfather Rai Bahadur Buta Singh, was not a notable person in town. He was a postmaster and his name has not remained. My mother hadn't talked about her father's house, and I hadn't asked. But before going to Pindi, I had asked my uncles to describe the houses.

The house they were born in, the one that belonged to Nanaji, was a two-storey house on Saidpur Road, closer to the city than Nanaji's house. One could see the Saidpur hills from the house. This house too had no number. They lived on the ground floor. Above them lived a doctor and his wife.

I found no trace of it. The building in the most likely spot was now a butcher's shop.

After my mother had given Baiji the jewellery, Bauji and Baiji had had a new house built to their plan around 1924 or 1925. It was a single-storey brick house, also on Saidpur Road, but further from the city and closer to Nanaji's *saraan*. Mama Swaran described it vividly, saying it was a house 16 yards wide and 16 yards long, that is, two *hathas*. It also had steps leading to a street on the side. The street had no particular name, but there was a board saying Kucha (street) Sardar Ganga Singh.

The house had a big black and white tiled verandah which opened to an inner courtyard. Mama Khojinder remembers a rope swing strung from a beam on the verandah of their house. The verandah was long enough for them to swing so high that their feet would touch the roof. The game was to see whether they could touch the roof with their feet on the second swing. And all the time, Baiji would be shouting at them that they would get hurt. This was the swing from which Mummy had jumped when her fiancé came for an unexpected visit.

There were papaya, orange and lime trees growing in the courtyard, something my mother always wanted to do in the Nizamuddin house she built in Delhi after Partition. In her father's house there were three main rooms. In the central bedroom, the big one, on one side was Bauji's bed and on the other was Baiji's bed. One of the rooms was a living room, with a high bed, a sofa, which got transformed into a bedroom at night, a bit like the living room in Dharamshala. To the right of the courtyard was the prayer room. There were also a few small store rooms. And there was of course the flat roof, where they slept in the summer.

At night, there were hurricane lanterns. The luxury item was a Titmar lamp which cost Rs 14 or Rs 15. In the mid-1920s, this was nearly one-seventh of Bauji's monthly pension of Rs 103. Electricity came much later, in Mama Khojinder's college days, in the mid-1930s. The radio they got around 1937 or 1938.

Even with these detailed accounts, I cannot find the house. I cannot find a lane which at one time was called Kucha Ganga Singh after my grandfather. There is no sign of the water pump either. All I can see are shops. I come back again to the road, dragging my host's son from a live telecast of an Indian-Pakistani test match. I need to find this house, for I know that Mama Khojinder, 53 years after Partition, still dreams of Rawalpindi, of their house, of my parents' house, of Dehra Khalsa. But I can see nothing that even remotely resembles their house. And anyway it is not this Saidpur Road that Mama Khojinder dreams about. Instead, I buy gold-embroidered cushion covers for them from Raja Bazaar as a little remembrance of Rawalpindi.

We go to Panja Sahib where my family most likely went, for it is only a few hours out of Rawalpindi. It is a place of pilgrimage associ-

ated with Guru Nanak Dev Ji, our first Guru. It is said his disciple
Mardana was thirsty. So Guru Nanak told him to go up the hill to get
water from a *pir,* a Muslim saint who was meditating. The *pir* said, "If
your Guru is so great, tell him to create the water." On hearing that,
Guru Nanak put his palm on the rock – the imprint is still there –
and water came from the rock.

It was with shame and embarrassment that I had to argue with
the Sikh gatekeepers to let my Muslim host and his son into the
Gurdwara. I told him that my host knew more Gurbani than I did.
Within the temple, there was the reading of the Holy Book. The
langgar, the communal meal, was being served outside. I sat down
in the line and had fried rice and vegetables. "Where do you come
from?" I asked a woman with gaily coloured clothes. The men wore
embroidered waistcoats. "We are from Swat", she said. I learnt for the
first time that there are Sikhs who remained in Swat in Pakistan.

No sense of having 'returned home'

I come away without any sense of having "returned home", without
feeling that I had walked the same roads my mother had walked.
Perhaps my mother never did walk the roads. Even in 2000, my
host does not like me to go out alone. The one time I have an official
appointment with the Director of Telecommunications, one of the
sons comes with me to the end of the road and deposits me in a taxi,
urging the driver to look after me. So it is that on my way back I make
a detour to visit the TB hospital in Rawalpindi. Mummy's mother
must have died at home, for the TB Centre in Rawalpindi was not
fully functional in 1911. But even now, when I visit the TB Centre
on Asghar Mall Road, there is a sense of dread. My first instinct
is to cover my mouth and nose with my *dupatta.* The dread only
worsens as I am taken on a guided tour and find that the facilities
include cremation and burial grounds. Even in 2000, TB was deadly
in Pakistan, with an estimated 100,000 people dying annually from
it. Women predominate 60:40 among TB patients. The man taking
me around says that malnutrition, neglect and the difficulty for men
in poor families taking time off from work to accompany the women

to the hospital are some of the reasons for this gender imbalance.

I go to the history books to learn about Rawalpindi but find little more than the bare facts. Rawalpindi is west of Kashmir, north of Lahore and east of the North West Frontier province, close to the ancient civilisation of Taxila. From 1765 to 1849 Rawalpindi was ruled by Sikh chieftains, but I learn little about the Ahluwalia *baradari* in Pindi. Its growth is linked to the establishment of a British cantonment, for Rawalpindi with its large tracts of infertile land was an important recruitment ground. It was the largest cantonment in northern India, according to Sir James Douie, writing in 1916. In 1911, Rawalpindi town was the fifth largest city in Punjab with 86,483 people. The ranking was Delhi, Lahore, Amritsar, Multan and then Rawalpindi. Sialkot, where my father's family had their home, was smaller than Rawalpindi at nearly 65,000.

I return from Pindi with memories of hospitality, of long talks at night with my host's daughter. I also return with questions, for the story I know of the place we left behind is full of silences and discordant notes. My mother did not talk of Rawalpindi much before I began probing. And even then, she did not want the curtain opened. She did not go back even when she could. She mourned the loss of the *khes* (thick woven bedclothes) and the clothes she had been collecting for her daughters' trousseaus. But other than Nuro, she never spoke of anyone left behind in Pakistan.

I also had few questions of her before I had seen Rawalpindi. It was only when I was sitting in my hostess' kitchen that I thought my mother would probably never have set foot in a Muslim kitchen. And my hostess, 50, or her mother, would never have known my mother or anybody in her circle. My hostess still keeps a strict *burka* and her infrequent accompanied forays out of the house are only to the house of kin.

Stories of pre-Partition India have been told mostly by educated, well-to-do men who lived in large cities. They speak nostalgically of close friendships across religious divides. From literature and the written history, I had formed the impression that Hindus, Sikhs and Muslims had a harmonious relationship till the madness of Partition overcame everybody. But these stories of pre-Partition society underplay the rigidity of caste and religious boundaries for men and women who did not have the money or education to flout them.

In Rawalpindi, caste controlled the relations between Sikh and Hindu neighbours in our middle-class neighbourhood. Bauji was particularly caste conscious, seeing himself as better than those around him. This was interesting, for the Bhagars, his caste, were not seen as a high group among the Sikhs.

Lata tells of a Hindu household opposite ours consisting of two sisters, Ram Pyari and Sumitra, who had married two brothers. This was in 1942 when Bauji, Mama Khojinder and his new bride were staying in our house while Mummy, Pitajee and Ranjan were in Karachi. These two sisters started coming to our home and became friends with my aunt. Their family were traders. Bauji did not think they were of equal status. Lata says:

> Bauji one day shouted at Mamiji, "Why do you talk so much to them?" She kept quiet. Unfortunately Sumitra got bone TB. Bone TB is not infectious but Bauji put his foot down that they were not to enter the house. What could she do? How could she tell them her father-in-law thought they were inferior to their family? She saw them again but only outside the house. She did not want them to be shouted at, for Bauji could have insulted them.

Lata says Mamiji asked her:

> Who is superior? They or us? Only three days ago, I had no money in the house. And I went to Ram Pyari and said, "I have no money. It is the end of the month. Do you have some?" "Bhabhiji", Ram Pyari said, "why did you have to ask? You should have just ordered me." And she opened her bag and it was full of Rs 100 notes, Rs 50 notes. They were in business, but never in our conversation had they indicated they had so much money. And now I am told I am superior to them.

In my mother's story, there is no mention of childhood friends, Hindu, Sikh or Muslim. Her childhood was populated by her brothers and cousins, her aunts and uncles, her mother and father, and her grandparents. It was framed by the Ahluwalia *baradari*. There is also nothing in her story as she told it to indicate that her father's house and her marital home were in a mixed Hindu, Sikh and Muslim area, or that Muslims comprised more than four-fifths of the population of Rawalpindi district.

Mama Swaran says there was a Muslim colony behind Saidpur Road. At one end of the road on which her marital home was located there was a mosque. On Saidpur Road there were many Sikh houses and a few Muslim houses also. The Sikh philosophy that all paths lead to the one God was perhaps behind my mother's emphasis on the inter-religious harmony that existed in Rawalpindi. Yet in her own life, Nuro was the only Muslim with whom she had a relationship. Even that was not a peer relationship, and we do not know how Nuro saw it.

But even having a Muslim masseuse was unusual in that neighbourhood. Mummy told Ritu Menon and Kamla Bhasin that Nuro "would have to lift the *chic* aside to enter... Well, my neighbours who were typical old-fashioned Hindus, they would say to us, you lift your *chics* and only then will we enter. Because they had been touched by a Muslim!"

Mummy, like other Sikhs, would not eat *halal* meat. That meant she would not eat in a Muslim house. This gap between the daily lived reality and the ideal of inter-religious harmony meant that when she wanted to emphasise the harmony, she would give the male perspective from Nanaji's time. When asked about Sikh–Muslim relations, she said:

In Rawalpindi we had very good relations with the Muslims, with their *pirs*. When my *nani* passed away the *pirs* read from the Qoran Sharif, we had a paath of the Guru Granth Sahib, of the Gita... people lived together because their culture was the same, their attitudes were similar... Hindus, Sikhs and Muslims were not divided then, they were not separate.

None of this was true for my mother's life. Perhaps it was true for her grandfather. My host had a photograph dating back perhaps to the early 1900s, which shows Rai Bahadur Buta Singh sitting with Deputy Commissioner Kitchener, Sh. Din Mohammad Advocate, Raja Sher Khan, and D.B. Daulat Rai. But there could not have been a similar photograph including the women.

Mummy recounted that her Nanaji "had exchanged turbans with the local elite Muslims to say that they were like brothers." "But", she says, "we never ate in their homes, our daughters never entered their house, theirs didn't come in ours… but the men were like brothers. We attended their weddings, they gave us dry rations, *mishri*".

But she recognised that even for the men, "the close relationship… was between us and a handful of well-off Muslims. But the majority were poor and they were exploited by us." This is particularly telling, for it was Muslims who tilled Bauji's land. It was the Muslim tenant's buffalo that ended up in Bauji's house when he could not pay his debt. I did not meet any Muslims from such a background to know how they felt about Partition. But Muslims like my host, who are nostalgic for the pre-Partition image of inter-religious harmony, come from landed families.

My uncles also did not have close Muslim friends. Mama Khojinder remembers that one of the Muslim boys, Noor Mohamad, was his friend and classmate. But Mama Swaran is more guarded. He says, "With Muslims we had reasonably good relations. We used to play with them. There was a Muslim family by the side of our house. There was no enmity." Then as an aside, Mama Swaran says that there was a sense of fear vis-à-vis the Muslims. It was a matter of comfort that there were other Sikh houses between them. He then mentions casually:

During the British time, quite often there used to be Muslim-Hindu riots. Two or three times I remember there were riots. We used to go to Rai Bahadur Buta Singh's *saraan*, for two, three families could be accommodated there. Jasbir [Mummy's first cousin but he was also related to them via Baiji] used to have guns – they all had guns. We used to take our dinner with us and spend the night there.

Sitting in my hostess' kitchen, I am again struck by the dominant divisions of religion and class. And yet the scene is so like the one my sisters and uncles describe in their memories of the city. The mother cooks in the kitchen, looking out over an inner courtyard with flowering vines. One by one the family members enter, sit down on low wooden platforms to have the *chapatis* hot from the iron griddle. We speak Punjabi, Rawalpindi style. And I think that in another time and place, my mother and my hostess would have understood each others' bounded lives in Rawalpindi.

After a week in Pakistan, I step back into India, take a deep breath, remove my *dupatta* from my head and hail a male taxi driver. I sit alone in the cab and tell him to take me to my uncle's house in Amritsar. When I go back to Delhi, Mama Swaran and I talk till 2 a.m. about the family's life in Pindi, in a way we never did before.

Chapter 6

Ecstasy and madness

———

I had always known that my mother regarded Bapuji as her father. I grew up thinking of Bapuji's children and their families in Delhi as my extended kin. But the rest of the story happened to a mother I did not know.

Amrit

Bapuji – his name was Mal Singh – came into Mummy's life in 1929 when he visited Rawalpindi with the *jatha*, his religious group. They held baptismal ceremonies where Sikhs partake of *amrit* (nectar) and take a vow of truthful living. Bapuji was one of four brothers and was born in Sarli, a village near Amritsar. But after serving in the First World War, he was given land in Ukarai, near Lyallpur. That is where he lived until Partition, when he was compensated with land in Tarn Taran.

Mummy's cousin and aunt – the aunt was Mummy's mother's brother's wife who used to live in Nanaji's house – had partaken of *amrit*. Seeing them, Mummy yearned for *amrit* too. They told her she would have to remove her jewellery. Moreover, a married couple had to be baptised together. Mummy agreed to removing her jewellery, but doubted that Pitajee would want to be baptised again as he had already taken *amrit*.

After the prayers, a group of them were walking Bapuji back to the house where he was staying. As he turned towards them to greet them with the traditional greeting, "*Waheguru ji ka Khalsa, waheguru ji ki fateh*" (The Khalsa belongs to God. Glory be to God), Mummy, then 18, got the courage to plead with Bapuji, saying, "Please make Doctor Sahib agree to it so that I can also have *amrit*." Mummy says, "Bapuji looked at me, his eyes full of light. He said, '*Bibi*, now I will put a shawl through your words and persuade him with humility and folded hands.'"

Bapuji and Pitajee, 1967

The next day Pitajee agreed to take *amrit*. Mummy had gone to another house for hymns when she got a message saying she should come home and get ready for the *amrit* ceremony. She says, "For me, it was as if the impossible had happened."

She asked Pitajee's permission to take off the ring he had given her at the time of their marriage. She took off the rest of the jewellery and kept it safe. Much of it was sold later during Pitajee's illnesses. To purify herself, she washed her hair and had a bath. Lata was less than a year old, so Mummy just put water on her head. Pitajee had greater problems, for he had got the runs. He had to bathe three times, for every time he went to the toilet he had to bathe again.

There were 20 to 25 people who were going to be initiated in that sitting. Men and women were sitting on opposite sides. The five *piarai*, the five beloved, read hymns while stirring the *amrit* in an iron pot.

Mummy says:

I couldn't believe that I was going to take *amrit*. People kept congratulating me that Doctor Sahib has agreed. I was silent. Humble. It was as if I was in total thankfulness. The five *piarai* [the beloveds] called me and asked me loudly, "Why are you here, Bibi?" I said, "To have amrit" and my eyes filled.

Bapuji said, "Start with the Bibi." As soon as I had one sip, I lost consciousness. I went into a trance. It was as if I was lost. There is strength in the *amrit*. It was as if I saw another spiritual world. I felt the atmosphere was different, that it was spiritual.

So started the relationship with Bapuji. She says, "In my mind arose a great hero worship of Bapuji. I did not speak to him, but within me there was a lot of respect and love, as if he were superhuman." Pitajee was also strongly drawn to Bapuji and asked him over for dinner at home. The next day, the hymns were sung in their home. Mummy says:

> The first time I did the *nitnem* [the daily prayers], the verse appeared that the *amrit* that the gods desire, that *amrit* I have received. It fitted me. I became very emotional, went into *virag* [desolate longing] and started crying.
>
> We came as it were into the front ranks. The three or four days that Bapuji stayed, he showed his attachment to us. He brought us into the limelight, particularly me. And he explained to Pitajee that she is an uplifted spirit, that you should cherish her. So in the morning, Pitajee started bowing before me.

She laughs, remembering it. "It had an effect on your father. If such a spiritual man says it, maybe it is true that I have a pure soul. I was then held in a bit of regard."

Manic

The religious excitement triggered a manic episode in Pitajee. His family turned against Mummy, saying she was the one who had made Pitajee get baptised. Mummy's father and mother were against the *jatha* too, seeing the link between this new immersion in religion, singing hymns all night and the onset of her husband's manic phase. They also thought that their daughter was not behaving normally. But Pitajee wanted Bapuji and the *jatha* to come back the next year in 1930 and stay and do an *akhand paath* in their house. The *akhand paath* is the continuous reading of the Guru Granth Sahib, the Sikh holy book. It is an intense three-day religious immersion. Bapuji was very worried, for he was afraid Pitajee would fall ill again.

Pitajee insisted. He wanted to make amends. In 1929, they had had an *akhand paath* at home. When Pitajee fell ill, he had interrupted the continuous reading by making the girl who was reading get up. So the *akhand paath* was no longer continuous. The break in the reading is seen as a great sin and, to compensate, you have to have another *akhand paath*. But Bapuji had to go away and so it remained incomplete for a year. Pitajee said his mind was greatly burdened by this transgression.

So Bapuji and the *jatha* again came to Rawalpindi in the summer holidays of 1930. Again Pitajee fell ill. Mummy was worried something terrible would happen. Pitajee would say his head was on fire. Bapuji's brother's son, Professor Thakur Singh, would leave the hymn singing and pour bucket after bucket of water on Pitajee's head. This was the year Professor Thakur Singh became part of Pitajee and Mummy's life. At the time he was in his early 30s and was teaching physical education at Ludhiana Government College. He was known in our family as Mamaji, Professor Sahib or Ludhianai walai (the person from Ludhiana).

One night everybody was sleeping on the terrace – Pitajee, Mummy, Lata, Dadijee and the people who had come for the *akhand paath*. Professor Sahib also slept there, on a bed next to Pitajee. Mummy was sleeping away from Pitajee for she was afraid. Pitajee went down and picked up the small sword worn by initiated Sikhs. Mummy was fast asleep. She says:

I woke up and he was standing over my head with the sword. It was the madness in him. I woke up with fright and said, "What is the matter, what's the matter?" By this time, Professor Sahib also got up. He said, "What are you doing, brother?" Pitajee said, "Friend, I was scaring her. I wasn't going to kill her."

Mummy went back to her father's house to stay, but her family turned more strongly against the *jatha*, seeing a link between the all-night hymn singing and Pitajee's illness.

It was time for the *jatha* to leave. Bapuji was worried. The first time they had come, Pitajee had fallen ill. The second time too he had fallen ill. Bapuji felt compassionate that the young woman was all alone. Then Ludhianai walai said to Bapuji, "People will say, they sing the hymns, eat the food at people's houses and go away". He added, "Bibi is so sad. We should also share some of her sorrow."

Bapuji said "Your words are very true, but I can't figure out whom to leave behind." All the others had jobs, but Professor Sahib had 15 to 20 days of leave left. Bapuji said, "The truth is, I don't trust anybody else. The girl is still young. If you stay, I will leave one other man with you."

And so Professor Thakur Singh and Bhau, a very strong man who used to play the *dholak* (drum), stayed with Pitajee for 15 days. Mummy continued to stay with her parents at night. She would go to her marital home in the morning and return in the evening. But after 15 days Professor Thakur Singh and Bhau had to go away. They wondered whether to take Doctor Sahib with them to Ludhiana. But he could run away from Ludhiana too. Mummy could not turn to her in-laws. Her parents also held her accountable. But her mother's brothers respected Bapuji. So she asked her mother's brother, Mama Atma Singh, for help and he sent two of his men to look after Pitajee for another 15 to 20 days.

Pitajee fell ill a third time. He got typhoid and went manic again in 1930. Mummy says, "I was frightened of the illness. The house would get uprooted, the world would turn upside down. Day after day, people couldn't come and stay in the house."

She was distraught. Her husband was gravely ill. But she had also come to love Bapuji like her father and people were speaking ill of him and the *jatha*. So she wrote a letter and asked her second cousin

Kirpal Singh, who was also the *jathedar* (the head of the group) of Rawalpindi, to take the letter to Bapuji. In the letter she wrote:

Jap tap sanjam dharam na kamaia
Sewa sadh na janiai har raiya
Kahu Nanak ham neech karma
Saran parai ki rakho sarma (Sodar rahras panna 12)

I have not practised meditation, penance, self control and
    truthfulness,
I have not served holy people and have not recognised God,
    the King,
Our deeds are mean, [pray like this] says [Satguru] Nanak,
[O my God], kindly preserve my honour, I seek Your shelter.
(Trans: Harbans Singh Doabia)

At that time Bapuji was in Tarn Taran. Bhai Randhir Singh, who was the leader of the *jatha*, was also there. He was part of the first wave of freedom fighters in the Punjab and was imprisoned from May 1915 to October 1930. He had just been freed from prison after 15 years, for being part of the Gurdwara Reform movement. He was honoured by Sikhs for his spirituality and struggle for religious reform.

After receiving the letter, Bhai Randhir Singh asked Bapuji to pray in the Tarn Taran Gurdwara, pleading, "True Lord have mercy. Make him well." The *hukumnama*, the reading for the day was very appropriate. The last four lines were

Hoi dayal kirpal prabhu thakur apai sunai bainti
Pura satguru mol milawai sabh chukai man ki chinti
Har har nam avkhaj mukh paiya
Jan Nanak sukh vasanthi

Becoming kind and compassionate, the Lord Master Himself
    hears my supplication,
He unites me in the union of the perfect true Guru and my

mind's cares are all dispelled.
The Lord God has put the cure-all of His Name into my mouth
and slave Nanak, now abides in peace.

(Trans: Manmohan Singh)

They sent Mummy the verses and the holy offering of sugar wafers.
With them came the instruction to meditate all day on the verses.
Within seven days, Mummy said, Pitajee became well again.

My mother and father's first meeting with Bhai Sahib Randhir
Singh was after yet another bout of illness, around 1933, after Pitajee
had a vision of Bhai Sahib. He saw Bhai Sahib Randhir Singh standing
by the window, talking to the superintendent of the mental hospital,
Colonel Lodge Patch. The doctor was saying, "He is mental, he is ill."
But Bhai Sahib was saying, "No. He is all right. He is well."

Pitajee had been unconscious before, but he got up and told them
his dream. He began to walk, though he was very weak. He wanted
to meet Bhai Sahib and Bapuji. So my mother and father, together
with my mother's aunt (the one who had introduced her to Bapuji)
and cousin Kirpal Singh, went for the first time to Bapuji's house in
his village near Lyallpur.

Bapuji received them very warmly and accompanied them to Bhai
Sahib's place in Narangwal. When Pitajee saw Bhai Sahib, he was
stunned. Mummy says:

He said, "Yes he was the man. Here at this window he was
standing. Here the doctor was standing." A supernatural thing
had happened. Your Pitajee went into a trance of devotion. But
he did not fall ill.

My mother met Bhai Sahib again. She went to Jalandhar for the
marriage of her cousin, the Pindi queen's son. All her maternal kin
were there. She had gone with her aunt, the same aunt who had been
baptised and was devoted to Bapuji and Bhai Sahib. As the groom's
party was staying at the bride's house for two days, Mummy and her
aunt decided to go to Narangwal and pay their homage to Bhai Sahib

Randhir Singh.

Mummy writes of this episode at length in the book in memory of Bapuji by Professor Thakur Singh. They left immediately, taking a bus to Ludhiana, went to Professor Thakur Singh's house and together with him went to Bhai Randhir Singh's house. They arrived after dark to find that Bhai Sahib had gone to Patiala and would not be back for three or four days. Mummy says:

I became very sad and went on crying that it is not in my destiny to meet them. We had only two nights there for it was important for Mamiji to be in Jalandhar before noon when the bridal party returned. And I could not stay there alone.

She writes, when she heard they were away:

My mind sank to impenetrable darkness. Hopelessness engulfed me...

Bhai Sahib's wife Kartar Kaur and his daughter Daler Kaur tried to console me, but how could my mind find peace? After the evening prayer, they placed me in the front to have my meal. With great effort I ate a few morsels. I did not want to talk to anybody. Everybody went to sleep but how can sleep come to eyes that are thirsty for meeting?

All night passed, aching, walking, pleading, "Oh God, giver of all, have pity. How can I meet him? Who knows when destiny will bring me here again... What You want You can do." Pleading, begging, dawn broke. After the bath, the hymns began. Slowly the day passed. Evening fell. This evening was full of deep despair.

All of a sudden, Bhai Sahib's daughter Bibi Daler shouted, "They've come. Father has come." Mummy could not believe it. She ran downstairs, and there saw Bhai Randhir Singh.

The glory of that meeting is indescribable. My head bowed with gratitude. He put both his hands on my head and said, "Bibi, we knew early this morning at *amrit* time, that you have come. I saw your desolation [*vairagh*]. Your mind's torment was such that we could not stay there any longer. I told Bauji [Bapu Mal Singh], "Let's go. Bibi Inder is waiting for us. She is very desolate."

With Bhai Sahib, Bapuji had also come. Mummy hadn't even known he was there. At night there was a lot of hymn singing. My mother too played the *iktara* and sang the hymns full of devotion and gratitude. At 11 p.m., the sitting was brought to an end. Food was served. Bhai Sahib and Bapuji showed her a lot of love and honour. The next day Professor Sahib accompanied them to Ludhiana and put them on the bus to Jalandhar.

My father fell ill once more in 1937. Again there was an *akhand paath* by the *jatha* in Mummy and Pitajee's home in Rawalpindi. The same pattern repeated itself. He was being guarded but escaped and went straight to the mental hospital in Lahore. There the doctors suggested giving him electric shock treatment, which was at an experimental stage at the time.

Mummy signed the consent form. Desperate for comfort she went to Ukarai to see Bapuji and Bhai Sahib. It was Bapuji's daughter's Gyan's wedding. There Mummy found Bapuji had been kicked by a mare and his skull was broken. She looked after him. It was this visit that bonded her with the rest of Bapuji's family.

On her way back to Rawalpindi, she sat with Bhai Sahib Randhir Singh Ji in the bus. All of a sudden, Bhai Sahib put his hand on Mummy's head, his eyes full of blessing. Bhai Sahib said, "Enough Bibi. Your suffering is over. Now Doctor Sahib will be well." Mummy bowed her head in thankfulness.

In Lahore the electric shock treatment had begun. Before they gave him the third electric shock, the family was allowed to see him. Pitajee slowly became better. My mother came to get him and they went to the Murree Hills.

The Mental Hospital on Jail Road

In Lahore I visit the Mental Hospital on Jail Road. My father stayed here twice when he became manic – once in 1930 and again in 1937.

Pitajee had no money on him but took a train, got thrown out, walked the rest of the way from Rawalpindi, took a lift. Nobody knows the full details of the story. He finally reached Lahore, 375 km away, which had the only mental hospital in Punjab. At the time it was called the Central Asylum for Lunatics. In 1996 its name was changed to the Government Hospital for Psychiatric Diseases, Lahore. It was built in Lahore at its present site in 1900 on 172 acres on Jail Road. The Superintendent of the Asylum also served as the Professor of Lunacy at the Lahore Medical College.

My father must have passed through two fort-like red gates to get to the male patients' section. Only one gate remains, for the front portion of the hospital is now occupied by the Punjab Institute of Cardiology. He must have passed by the opium factory to the right which had already encroached on hospital land and continues to produce opium pills. Maybe he noticed the flower beds with cockscombs, cosmos, roses and nasturtiums on the left side of the road or the jasmine bushes on the right. Most likely, at that time there were also orange groves and locquat trees.

In 1930, the Superintendent of the Asylum was Colonel Lodge Patch, who headed the hospital from 1922 to 1947. There had always been a closeness between my father and this professor, for my father had won the medical college gold medal for excellence in the study of mental diseases when he graduated in 1923. My father used to tell the story with great delight, that the professor had wondered how he could have such a great insight into mental disease. My father told him it was because he himself suffered from it.

The story goes that the peon wouldn't let my father into the hospital. Pitajee said, "You just tell the Superintendent that Pargat Singh has come." While he was shouting at the peon, the superintendent came out. The minute he saw him, Pitajee said, the superintendent burst out crying. He could not stop crying, seeing his brightest student come to this. He would not believe that Pitajee was ill.

Colonel Lodge Patch called for my mother's uncle in Lahore, Masi Jasram's husband. The superintendent was very angry and said, "You are not looking after this very intelligent student. He is all right. You are calling him mad." Pitajee was inside. He took the tape from his underwear and tried to hang himself with it. Only then was the superintendent willing to believe that Pitajee was seriously ill. He remained there for a month.

The advantage of the hospital was that the manic patient could be controlled and there was regular medication. However, the main way of controlling the patient was "chaining" him or her. This meant locking the patient in the cell or at other times chaining the patient to a tree. One of the doctors in the hospital says he believes hydro-therapy was also used – dousing the patient with a strong jet of water.

Pitajee fell ill once more in 1937. He was shut up at home in the mezzanine room with a window. Two people were keeping guard over him. But Pitajee was a doctor himself and knew that he should be in the mental hospital. While they were asleep, he ran away. Though all the doors were closed, he hung a sheet on the balcony of the prayer room and dangled on it outside and went down. He went straight to the mental hospital in Lahore.

In the 1930s, the standard treatment for manic patients was to give them medication to render them weak and unconscious. The other option was to tie the patient down and lock him or her in the house. Before treatment with lithium became standard, manic-depressive psychosis was difficult to control. Electric shock treatment was then at an experimental stage. A consultant psychiatrist at the hospital in January 2000, Dr Asghar Ali, says it was most likely used without anesthesia. My mother was told that when the pulse got weak, they stopped it. Before they gave my father the third electric shock, the family was allowed to see him.

Lata, who was eight at the time, remembers he took them to a garden and gave them oranges, most likely from the orange groves that Lodge Patch had had planted. His room was light and airy, with very little furniture. Following her description, I go with Dr Ali to the older portions of the hospital, the *purana jangala*, which was built in 1900 for Indian male patients.

It is a two-storeyed block. It is large. There seemed to be nearly a hundred rooms built around a large quadrangle with arches on the verandahs marking each room. The verandahs of the second storey are barred. The rooms used to be indeed empty of furniture, just about capable of accommodating two people. There were no beds with white sheets and red blankets at the time. The patients used to sleep on cotton or husk mattresses. Only when Dr Ali points out the relative newness of the toilets do I realise that the old wards had no toilet facilities for patients. Not even for the doctors, clarifies Dr Ali.

In the centre of the quadrangle is a large garden with a grove of trees, including some old *barh* trees (*Ficus bengalensis).* There are benches dotted throughout, the kind my sister remembers. Some of these trees are now so old that they have fenced platforms around them, invaluable for their shade in the summer.

Pitajee could also have been in the new wards, for they were completed in 1937. Lodge Patch had introduced open wards for the first time. It had the same structure as the old wards, the same kind of doors and iron bars, the same kind of garden, except that only three sides of the quadrangle were built.

Both the buildings used to be red brick, though the old one has just been painted white. Each of the rooms has a grey-blue, solid iron door with a peephole. The room also has a window with six stout iron bars. Inside this is a door with another six bars which is also locked. The lock on this door clangs with an air of finality. As one of the attendants demonstrates how the bolt goes into the door, I shiver. The sound of this door clanging shut must have remained with my father forever.

Half a banana

Mummy and Pitajee started out together in their attachment to Bapuji and Professor Thakur Singh, through ecstasy and madness. But in time my father was no longer part of this inner circle, though he was much honoured by Bapuji and Professor Thakur Singh. The connection between Mummy and Bapuji was so strong that it also excluded her parents, brothers and her in-laws.

The religious part of Mummy, the part that belonged to Bapuji and his family, did not belong to her children. Lata and Ranjan, who remember this early period of religious immersion, saw it as something that made both Mummy and Pitajee forget their children's welfare, leaving them open to physical neglect and sexual abuse. Lata says:

> With the *jatha* coming in, Ranjan and I were very neglected. When the *jatha* came to town, Mummy lost consciousness of her children. They used to leave us at home. We used to have male cooks at home who then tried to sexually molest us. We had no understanding when they put their hands here and there. We put [the blame] on the *jatha*.
>
> We told Aijee. We told Pitajee also. What kind of prayers are these when you neglect your small children? They had both become carried away over this. The *simran* that they do [praying with every breath], sometimes they would do it for an hour. They would do it in our house, in other people's houses. When there were two people, they would do *Wahai Guru, Wahai Guru*. I would think it is part of sex also, if a man and a woman did it.

Lata's searing memory is when the *jatha* was visiting Sialkot and Pitajee and Aijee took the girls and went with the *jatha* to Sialkot. Lata got up in the morning to find both her parents gone. She says:

> I remember it so vividly. Ranjana was sleeping but I could not find Aijee or Pitajee. Outside there was a man who said they had gone 40 miles away with the *jatha*, and they had told him to take us to Bhuajee's house. Bhuajee used to live in Sialkot, where they had a small hotel.
>
> I got ready and got Ranjan ready. The man took us and told Bhuajee that Aijee Pitajee had gone to a prayer meeting. Bhuajee asked, "When will they come back?" He said, "They will be back in the evening." She fed us, gave us lunch and tea in the evening. Then she sent us back in the rickshaw.
>
> It was 6 o'clock, 7 o'clock, 8 o'clock, 9 o'clock. No Aijee Pitajee.

No servants. Only the *sardar* outside. 11 o'clock. Ranjan became frightened. She was so small. I can still hear her crying, "Lata, I am very hungry". I saw there was a window and on a white plate, there was one banana. First I gave her half the banana. I was also hungry. Then Ranjan said, "Lata, I am still hungry." I gave her the other half.

I don't remember whether I had water or did not have water. She went to sleep. She was small. That I have not forgiven, ever. Aijee and to some extent Bhuajee also. [With] small, small children, at least you should make sure their parents have come home.

Somehow, this stupid kind of worship, I associated with this banana. I could never take to the *jatha*. The minute Aijee heard the *jatha kirtan*, she would start crying and keep crying. Somehow I could never take to Professor Sahib also because he was part of the *jatha*. I believe in God but became anti-religious.

Ranjan too has her own stories of the way the religious setting led to sexual abuse. She says that she is religious in her own way, but she too has no use for rituals or organised religiosity. She tells how one day one of the persons deeply honoured for his spirituality was visiting them in Delhi. This was when we were in the Lodhi Estate one-bedroom unit. Mummy had directed a play in Miranda House based on the romantic tragedy "Sohni Mahiwal". Mummy stayed behind, but Pitajee, Ranjan and I and our visitor came back earlier. Pitajee went to sleep in the bedroom. And outside in the verandah which was screened by bamboo blinds, this man put his tongue inside Ranjan's mouth, his hand under her tunic and felt her all over. Ranjan was 20 at the time. Ranjan says:

You were sleeping. Everybody was sleeping. And this drama was going on here. Aijee only came at 12 p.m. I was genuinely worried that Aijee hadn't come. Let him stop. I couldn't really find a way to communicate what had happened to me. The guy either didn't know what he was doing or he knew I wouldn't talk.

Whenever I saw him, I did the usual obeisance. He was a very good man. But this kind of a play was totally foreign to him. I lost a tremendous amount of respect for all these religious people. I realised that under all this religious fervour there is a tremendous amount of sexuality. How do I know what goes on in their lives?

When I was growing up in Delhi, we did not have the hymn singing and *akhand paaths* at home. The *jatha* did not come to stay. My mother's life was full of teaching and studying, trying to survive. Most of the time we did not have a prayer room in the temporary accommodation in Delhi after Partition. In Khyber Pass, where we did have a prayer room, I was expected to do the daily obeisance. Pitajee once said I should sit and listen to the recitation of our holy book. I told him I did not understand what was being recited. He got furious and ordered me to listen. I did not willingly go to the Gurdwara and listen to the recitation or hymns for the next 40 years. And anyway, one day the roof fell down in the prayer room and there were no more prayers in that room.

Life of the spirit

Bapuji's family for me meant periodic visits by Bapuji and Professor Thakur Singh to our home in Delhi. I also went with my mother to visit Bapuji's daughter and son, Gyaan and Harbans and their families who lived in Delhi. It is with Bindi, Masi Gyaan's son, and Nikki, Mama Harbans' daughter, that I still have a relationship, even after spending more than half my life away from India. But even as a child I remember their ways as different. My one lasting memory of visiting Mama Harbans is seeing a number of men sitting on *charpoys* (rope beds) in their *kachas,* the long underwear that is supposed to be worn by Sikh men and women.

I was embarrassed to see half-dressed men sitting outside and remember my mother saying, "So what? They are wearing *kachas.*" But I had never seen anyone in my family sitting like that in public, and it seemed to me to mark the difference between urban and rural ways, and something distinctive perhaps of the Jats, the landholding caste to which Bapuji and his family belonged.

My mother's life of the spirit was something personal and private. She would meditate in the morning – what I used to call her bottoms-up pose – head down while sitting cross-legged on the bed. We all thought that sometimes she was asleep. She did not press her religious practice on to me, possibly pedalling softly in contrast to my father. Now, there are times when I wish I could ask her about meditation in our religious context. Not learning Gurmukhi and not learning to read Gurbani also has left me feeling particularly unlettered of late. It also influenced the way I did not pressure my children into religious practice. Particularly when my elder son became a born-again Christian, I wondered whether I had been responsible for him not feeling rooted in our religion.

My mother's only religious requirement of me was that I go with her to Sis Ganj Sahib Gurdwara on the birthday of our first teacher, Guru Nanak Dev Ji. It meant getting up at 4 a.m. on a wintry morning in November, having a bath, then taking two buses to Chandni Chowk and walking to Sis Ganj Sahib. We would place our shoes in the shoe area, offer our obeisances, then walk barefoot to the large tents which accommodated hundreds of thousands of Sikhs from all over Delhi.

My mother wanted to reach the Gurdwara in the early hours of the morning to listen to the hymns. She would go into her familiar pose, head buried deep down, every now and again wiping her eyes and nose, for she cried listening to the hymns. Embarrassed, I would sit behind, knowing that it would be an hour or two. By 8 a.m. the crowd would begin to swell. The atmosphere would change from one of quiet religious devotion and fervour to that of a public mêlée.

We would then go out, and the first stop would be the stall selling hot fried chickpea flour balls served with grated radish and chillies on a plate made of dried leaves. Then we would give our token to retrieve our shoes from the communal shoe storage – separate lines for men and women. The next stop was at the corner of Sis Ganj Sahib where the best *jalebis* in the world were sold. You could watch the golden spirals being fried then dunked in syrup. Three *jalebis* in a leaf plate cost 12 annas. That was expensive in the late 1950s but it was our birthday treat.

My mother told me how she felt a yearning for God, how she felt lost and rudderless if she could not hear *gurbani* (the songs of God). I listened to her, thinking her language was unnecessarily flowery and sentimental. Then after her death, I discovered her writings about Bapuji and Bhai Sahib Randhir Singh in the two books I did not even know she had partly written with Professor Thakur Singh.

As I read her words on the page, I discovered I had not understood this deep core of her being. She had told me the story of the *panjiri*, semolina roasted in *ghee* and full of nuts and raisins. But I thought it was another instance of her born-again mentality which had become stronger as she grew older. I also judged her and the *jatha* as going against the philosophy of Sikhism. The Sikh faith holds equality before God at its centre and does not believe in caste. Sikhs demonstrate this equality by eating together at the Gurdwara.

The background to the *panjiri* story is that in reality Sikhs have caste, including an untouchable caste. There is also a caste-like division between initiated and non-initiated Sikhs. Initiated Sikhs of the *jatha* do not eat food prepared by the uninitiated. My mother was never prepared to discuss this contradiction between Sikh philosophy and practice.

The *jatha* held this ritual purity and pollution relating to food as central to their practice of Sikhism. Bhai Sahib Randhir Singh would not eat from the hands of Sikhs who had drunk wine, eaten meat or led an un-Sikh life. He kept to this even when he was in prison. When he was not allowed to prepare his own food or have it prepared by a "brother Sikh", he fasted or ate fruit when it was available. He ate only when the food was cooked by a Sikh who lived according to the principles of the faith.

When my father went to war, he infringed one of the rules of the initiated Sikhs – to abstain from eating meat. To purify himself, he and my mother would again have to be initiated again. For my mother, this meant that Bhai Sahib Randhir Singh Ji and Bapuji would not eat food cooked by her hands. But she thought if she took dry flour and roasted it in *ghee* with ground sugar and almonds, maybe they would eat this *panjiri*. She put the *panjiri* in a new vessel and placed it in their food cupboard. She informed the people who were in charge of the food, but they told her, "Bibi, you are not pure. Bhai Sahib and Bapuji will not accept this *panjiri*."

Her heart dimmed. When the *jatha* returned, *kirtan* started. Half the night passed. Then Bhai Sahib said, "Jogni [she who meditates on the glory of God], now bring the *panjiri*. Who says we will not have the *panjiri* made with your hands? Get up and bring the *panjiri*." With trembling hands, Mummy put the *panjiri* in an iron vessel and presented it. Quiet descended on the congregation. The hymns stopped. Bhai Sahib had two morsels of the *panjiri* and the hymns continued till noon the next day.

Mummy had told me the *panjiri* story, but I had not understood its emotional significance. However, she had not told me that Bapuji sent a letter to her college in Patti, a few years before his death, marked "Confidential". She writes of this in the book honouring Bapuji. In the letter, Bapuji told her that for a long time he had looked inside himself to find out why he felt such a pull of love and closeness to her. All of a sudden, he became sure that in a past life she had been his mother and he had been her son. He was very ill as a baby and she, his mother, had taken him to the Gurdwara, pleading with God that her life be taken to spare her child. And so it happened. That is why her love in a past life enfolds him and he sees her as his mother rather than as his daughter. That is why he said to her many times, "Give me your mother's love. But because you love me as a father, you have not understood." And so it was, he told her, that when she was gravely ill in Amritsar in 1970, at the *akhand paath*, he had pleaded, "Oh my Lord, give my beloved child more time for service and worship".

My mother had not spoken of this to anybody till she wrote about it after Bapuji's death in 1979. She had not spoken of it to us in Delhi, fearing our lack of understanding. To her and to everybody else in Bapuji's family, it made sense that their love and closeness was rooted in past lives.

I grew closer to Bapuji's family in Punjab after Mummy's death. I used to visit Amritsar when Mummy lived there and so would visit

Banta Bhainji, Bapuji's daughter's daughter, and Mama Kulwant, Bapuji's son. But Tarn Taran was not familiar territory. When my mother died, we went to immerse her bones and ashes in the river Beas near Goindwal Sahib, a historic Gurdwara an hour or so away from Tarn Taran. We then went to Tarn Taran Sahib for the prayer after the immersion. Lata said we could not visit Tarn Taran and not go to Bapuji's house. Bapuji was dead but his two sons still lived there. So we went to the elder son's house. It was already dark and they offered us fried and stuffed bitter gourd.

Bapuji's younger son, Joginder, who lived next door, also came to greet us. We were about to leave and Lata was already in the car, but Mama Joginder took Ranjan and me through a door and alley to a courtyard and then to an enclosed room. He pointed to the bed, saying, "This is where Bapuji was sitting one evening. He told me, Don't forget. This is Bibi Inder's *paikai*'." Mama Joginder began to cry, for he took the injunction seriously that this was Bibi Inder's maternal home, a home to which she has a perennial right. To make sure she could come and stay if she wanted, Mama Joginder had had a modern toilet built as Mummy could not squat.

He continued, "This is Bapuji's house. This is Bibi Inder's *paikai*. Daughters, this is your *paikai* too." He wanted us to promise that whenever we came to Punjab we would visit. He cried again, "Bapuji and Bibi Inder will be watching us, will be watching to see whether I am honouring my pledge."

Mummy's first death anniversary prayers were held in Bapuji's house. And I have been going back every year.

Chapter 7

Our stories of Partition

My mother was 36 when India was partitioned. I was three. For me, as for others of my generation in Punjab, stories of the Partition of British India to create independent India and Pakistan have formed the backdrop to family history. Things happened either before Partition or after Partition.

Partition was such a cataclysmic event that written history and literature have focused on the months before and after. Ten million were made homeless. One million died. Seventy-five thousand women are thought to have been abducted and raped. We were fortunate, for we left Karachi in 1948 and were safe. Mama Khojinder and Mama Swaran were already on the Indian side of the new border. Bauji was with Mama Khojinder in Ferozepur. On Nanaji's side, Mama Jaidev and Mama Atma Singh and their families were settled in Delhi. On my father's side, his sisters and brothers were also in India.

The unspoken story, however, has to do with the effects of Partition on marriage and family, on the shrinking of the kinship network, on changing roles, on education and paid work for women, on social and physical mobility. This is the story that would play out in my mother's life and mine. Partition was the catalyst for the unravelling that was still to take place in our family.

I don't remember people discussing any of these issues as they met and talked of Partition. What I heard again and again were our mythic stories of flight and resettlement. What is unusual in our story is that Mummy, having made it out safely to Bombay, went back alone to Karachi, retrieved my father's clinical instruments, sold the furniture and came back safely yet again.

"Hindus and Sikhs have lived together for centuries"

We moved to Karachi in January 1947. Though talk of Partition was in the air, my father discounted it. He argued that Muslims and

89

Sikhs had lived together for centuries. We were neighbours. We had a common history. So even if there was an India and a Pakistan, we would continue to live in Pakistan. After all, weren't there Sikhs in Afghanistan? Like many others, my father used to say that governments may change but people don't change. Mummy agreed with the decision. They had been happy in Karachi. Their world was now broader than the kinship-bounded world of Rawalpindi. So my father took his severance pay from the Army and opened a clinic in Karachi.

Mummy took Lata and Ranjan to Lahore to study – Lata at Kinnaird College for Women and Ranjan at the Ganga Ram School. But in May 1947, riots started in Lahore. Professor Thakur Singh's son-in-law took the girls to Ludhiana. Then Professor Thakur Singh brought them back to Karachi. He got back on the last safe train to India.

On the afternoon of 14 August 1947, my family was in the second row on the lawn of the Governor-General's House in Karachi, watching Mohammad Ali Jinnah, accompanied by his sister Fatima, accepting independence from Lord Mountbatten. They then went to a neighbour's house to listen to the radio and follow the news of Indian Independence scheduled for the following day.

The atmosphere was idealistic. Mummy said, "Two countries were formed. There was nothing to differentiate one from the other in people's minds." Ranjan remembers people saying, "The air of a free country is different." People in Karachi were able to relish the feeling at least momentarily. Karachi was far from the north-west frontier where troubles had already started. Dehra Khalsa, Bauji's ancestral village near Rawalpindi, was one of the first places to be destroyed.

Mami Mohinder, Mama Khojinder's wife, remembers that she skipped that particular news item when she read the papers to Bauji, whose eyesight had been failing. He noticed something amiss. Later in the day he heard on the radio that Dehra Khalsa had been razed to the ground. Mama Khojinder says:

His blood pressure rose. Bauji said, "There I was born. There I was raised. It was there I had my people. There I had my land, my house. Dehra Khalsa has gone. Everything has gone."

A month later, Bauji died.

We remained in Karachi for nearly six months after Independence. We lived in a double-storey house in a Muslim neighbourhood. Life continued with its daily routines. Every night after dinner the family would go for a walk, as they had done in Rawalpindi.

The troubles in Karachi seemed to begin all of a sudden. Ganda Singh, in his diary of Partition Days, writes that on Thursday, 6 January 1948:

A mob of some 25,000 (about 8,000 according to Pakistan official figure [sic]) Muslims attacked the Sikhs in a Gurdwara near Ratan Talao, Karachi, within half a mile of the Pakistan secretariat, followed by a wholesale massacre. The Gurdwara was set on fire and subjected to plunder. Not a single Sikh escaped with his life.

Mummy remembers it happened sooner. She says:

It erupted all of a sudden. It wasn't as if the tension grew slowly. It happened suddenly that there was news of killings… News came that somebody had killed a Sikh near the post office, in the area where your Pitajee had his shop. All of us panicked that it could be your Pitajee. There was immediate tension. Immediate.

Eight to ten days of tension followed. When the family went for their after-dinner walk, people stared. Mummy says, "I told your Pitajee, 'There seems a difference in the way people are looking at us. We shouldn't go outside.' He said, 'No, it is all in your mind. So what? Does anybody have the guts to harm us?'"

Soon after, one of the neighbours stopped Pitajee when he was alone and said, "Don't take the girls with you on your walk." Lata says:

We started getting the feeling that something would go wrong.

Neighbours started asking us, "You will have to leave very soon. Why don't you give the keys to us? My brother needs space, my sister needs a place." One person wanted to pay us for the house and all our furniture. But Pitajee said, "I will give the key back to the landlord."

My father still could not believe that Sikhs and Muslims could turn on one another. Mummy's second cousin Sharan, from Bauji's side, was then with the Pathan Police and posted to the Karachi air force station. A shot was fired at the Air Force station. Sharan came to get our family the next day. But Pitajee decided to stay put, saying their leaving would only add to the tension.

Sharan said, "Sister, he does not know. The tension is increasing day by day and you are staying in a very bad area." At this, Mummy said to Pitajee, "If you don't want to go, I also won't go. We'll keep the child, but let us send the two girls." Lata was 18, Ranjan was 14. They went with Sharan with their good clothes in two trunks.

"Mamaji, look before you shoot"

Sharan's place was about 12 miles away. He lived in the Air Force compound, surrounded by his loyal Pathan friends. As soon as Lata and Ranjan arrived there, Sharan had guards posted around the house.

Even after the girls were sent to Sharan's house, Pitajee was not worried. Their Muslim neighbour upstairs said to them, "Men have gone mad. How can you trust them?" They were indirectly telling us to leave. But Pitajee stayed.

The next day the Hindu ex-Mayor of Karachi came to see them. He was a friend of Pitajee's younger brother, Sanmukh. He told Mummy, "Bhabhiji [sister-in-law], I want you to move if you have a place to go." He tactfully told my father, "Even if there is a five per cent risk, why should you take it? If you don't go, it means Bhabhiji does not go, the child does not go. Leave your possessions here. Just take your clothes and go."

According to Ranjan, the clincher came when Mummy and Pitajee were going to the shop. I suppose that I must have been with them. Some people stopped them and said, "Please don't go further. Riots are going on." Right opposite Pitajee's shop, a Sikh had been killed. When Pitajee found he couldn't even go to his shop, he gave the key back to the Hindu landlord and decided to leave.

The next day, Mummy, Pitajee and I went to Sharan's house by bus, taking with us one or two boxes with four changes of clothes, some bedding and the jewellery that was left. Mummy said, "We thought when things go back to normal we will come back. We locked the house with all the furniture and utensils and came away."

The day we left the troubles began. The very next day there was looting in the area. Fires broke out. Our house was not looted because Muslims lived on the floor above. Girls were abducted. Our friends were sure that Doctor Sahib and Doctriani Sahib had been killed and the girls abducted. They recited the final prayers for our souls.

Mama Swaran, who was in the Indian Air Force, heard the news that Karachi had erupted. He told his senior officer that his sister and family were trapped in Karachi and he was allowed to bring a plane over to take us to safety. But when he reached Karachi, we had already moved to Sharan's house. He did not know where we were and returned with an empty plane.

We stayed with Mama Sharan for eight or nine days. My father's younger brother, Sanmukh, had been writing to him to come to Bombay. The north was impassable. So the only option was to go by ship to Bombay. Yet my father did not feel the situation was desperate. Ranjan says:

At first Pitajee said we could only afford a second-class ticket. At that time there were only first-class tickets available. We didn't have the money. Pitajee said, "What is the hurry? We'll wait for the second-class tickets."

But Mama Sharan was becoming nervous about the loyalty of his own Pathans. News about atrocities in India was becoming known in Karachi. So one day the most dramatic conversation took place. Aijee said, "See Sharan. If a mob comes, I give you full authority to shoot the girls." I was listening and said, "Mamaji, before you shoot, look carefully to make sure there is a mob." I thought I was cracking a grand joke. Mama Sharan left and burst out crying.

It had become clear that we had to leave so that Sharan could also leave and look after his family. He asked us to take his widowed sister's sons with us. By this time only tickets for the deck passage were available and we took those.

Mummy went back to the house in a police car with Pathan sepoys to get more of their goods. This is when she must have brought the old wooden box that we still have and the large tin trunk that used to be in Amritsar – one of those that can hold seven sets of quilts and mattresses. She says:

> Your Pitajee couldn't go with us, for they were killing Sikhs. But you couldn't tell with women. Not all the women wore burkas there. I was the only woman and sat with the driver, with the Pathans behind. We went to the house. We brought the bedding, the utensils, five or six boxes. On the way when the car stopped, people stared because a woman was sitting in the front. The driver started the car in a rush. There was a fair bit of a risk that they could have killed me or a fight could have erupted.

Sharan had the luggage sent to the ship, while the family went by bus accompanied by the Pathans. When they reached the ship, there were separate lines for men and women. Mummy carried me on. When she looked behind, Lata and Ranjan were not there. My mother says:

> My heart failed. I gave you to a person there and you screamed and screamed. If somebody had held on to their arms and moved them aside, what would we do? There was only a small line left. They were right at the back. I asked them, "Why are you standing at the back?" They said, "What can we do? People are pushing us." Then my life came back and I took the girls on board the ship.

Sharan wrote saying that when he went back by bus, it was the Pathans who saved him. The people in the bus said, "How come this *Sikhra* is on the bus?" The Pathans said, "He is our *Sardar*. Do not touch him." After we left, he and his family moved to Delhi. Nine years after Partition, we found ourselves living in the same compound in Khyber Pass in Delhi.

The journey from Karachi to Bombay took two nights and two days. Mummy remembered it as having been a difficult journey. People were vomiting. The toilets below were full of water. Ranjan remembers it as a grand adventure. They were on the deck and called it the first-class deck. Five Pathans accompanied them to the crowded ship. Mama Sharan came. The Pathans were so tall that they were able to hand us the trunks from the side of the ship. They got us settled in the bow of the ship.

Ranjan says, "We had blankets and we were eating and drinking the entire time. I remember getting lime pickle from somebody. It was a whole lime. It was like a picnic. Everybody was sharing their food."

I nearly fell. Everybody kept saying that if anything had happened to me, Chachaji (father's younger brother) would have been so disappointed, for Chachaji was very fond of me. When we reached Bombay, a lot of people were waiting there. Sikhs and Hindus would meet every ship that came in to check whether their friends had got out. As our family came out, we were greeted by people from the *jatha*. Ranjan says:

Everybody gave us such a grand welcome. All the Sikhs said, "*Shukar hai*, you have arrived. *Shukar hai*." Later, we found there had been a rumour that a doctor and his wife and three children had been killed on a train.

On the move

We went to Chacha Sanmukh's house. Ranjan remembers he had two rooms. It could have been his office, where he also lived. He had made a kitchen outside for us. There was a common bathroom for all the shops on the floor. It was right near Victoria Terminus, in the centre of Bombay. Trams would go clang, clang all day and night. You had to shout to talk. "But we got used to it", she says.

We stayed with Chachaji for two, two-and-a-half months. In Bombay, the *pagri* (the sweetener cum down-payment) for a shop for Pitajee's clinic was Rs 40,000 to Rs 80,000. We only had Rs 5000 or Rs 6000. Even that money was dwindling. Then Mama Jaidev Singh – Mummy's mother's brother from Nanaji's first marriage – called Pitajee to Delhi. Lata left with him.

Now that everyone was safe, Mummy wanted to go back and get Pitajee's surgical instruments. She was convinced that Pitajee could not practise without these instruments. She feared that they would not be able to replace them. She also wanted to sell the furniture. Pitajee had already gone to Delhi. His brother, Sanmukh, objected, saying that if anything happened to her, his brother would not let him be in peace. But my mother insisted. Sanmukh did not want to have anything to do with this adventure. He did not go with Mummy to the airport. She was obstinate. "No, I wasn't afraid of getting raped", she says. "I don't know, I had little fear."

Ranjan remembers that the airfare to Karachi was about Rs 260. There was a naval officer who had a bit of a crush on Ranjan. Mummy asked him to take her to the ticket office. She asked him to bring the money for the fare also. We probably paid him back later.

My mother was on the waiting list. When her name was not called, she told the booking people, "I have very important work in Karachi. I am going alone. You send me there whichever way you can." After a while they said, "Send in your luggage." Mummy says:

It was the first time I had travelled by air. There was a Mussalman sitting next to me. I said, "Bhai Sahib, Bhai Sahib", and told him I wanted to go to the Sindhan's house, where we had stayed first in a bungalow. He said, "Yes, of course. You are my sister, I will take you there." I don't know what he used to do. Our acquaintance was as seat companions only.

When they reached Karachi, there was a commotion because one of the passengers could not find his large trunk. After a while he was told that the trunk was coming in a later plane. Forty years later, Mummy laughs at the memory of taking the place of a trunk.

From my mother's perspective, the trip was a success. She brought back my father's surgical and medical instruments. She sold the furniture and it more or less covered the fare. But while she was in Karachi, tensions rose. She had moved from the Sindhan's house to the house of a Superintendent of Police, Sanmukh's friend. In India, trouble broke out in Junagarh, with Hindus killing Muslims. It became explosive in Karachi. Tickets out of Karachi were hard to get.

Ranjan used to study with a girl in Meerut whose father was a Major General in Karachi. Mummy phoned him. The Begum invited her to stay with them. But my mother did not want to go to a Muslim house, for "the eating drinking is different". Finally the General was able to obtain a first-class ticket on the black market for Rs 500. "I very much enjoyed coming back first class", Mummy said. All in all, for her, it had been worth it.

Mama Jaidev Singh invited the rest of the family to come and stay with him in Civil Lines, Old Delhi. We stayed there for seven or eight months. Lata says that at first we ate with them, then later we did our own cooking. Mama Jaidev saw us all cooped up in one room, so he gave us a huge tent in which to live and another tent where we did our cooking, and one bathroom in the bungalow. He said, "This is my sister's daughter and her family must be well looked after."

Mama Jaidev insisted that we stay with him until we could make other arrangements. His son Amarjit was going away to a hill station so we moved to Amarjit's place in Sujan Singh Park. Mama Jaidev came to visit us on the second or third day and said to Mummy, "Inder, don't ever think that I have sent you away. You wanted to move. After Amarjit comes back, if there is no arrangement, you come back to me."

Through Uncle Amarjit we learned that while the Ambassador Hotel was still under construction, refugees were being allowed to stay in the rooms that were ready. There was a shop available nearby.

Pitajee's was the only clinic. Soon, enough money began to come in for food. Money must still have been tight but we were at last living on our own.

There was a garden in front of the hotel that was hemmed in by shrubs, where the children of the "refugee block" would play together. One day a Muslim girl called Syeda who lived in one of the more substantial houses to the side of the hotel – her father was an important official in the education ministry – said that she wanted to catch butterflies with us. But the children, including me, pushed her out, saying we don't play with Muslims.

I came home and boasted about the incident. My father was upset. That evening, my father put on his formal black *achkan*, the long Muslim-style coat. My father, mother and I went to Syeda's house. In the dark hallway, we rang the bell. When Syeda's father invited us in, my father in his polite Urdu said, "We have come to apologise for what my child said to your daughter."

Syeda's mother joined us. We sat for a while having tea and sweet-meats. For Syeda's parents and mine, this must have been an attempt to recapture the notion of the gracious coexistence of Muslims and Sikhs and to overcome the brutality of Partition.

It isn't as if Syeda and I became friends. There was too much social distance between us. Her father was a senior government official and my family was struggling to survive. We caught up with each other years later at Miranda House at the University of Delhi. Once we were even part of the same debating team. But after acknowledging that we had shared some childhood memories, we never talked about that day.

Chapter 8

The graduation photograph

Mummy's black and white graduation photograph hung on the whitewashed wall in the living room of her Nizamuddin house in 1994, along with Nanaji's photograph. It showed my mother in a sombre pose, wearing a saree, holding her Master's degree in Punjabi literature. She was standing under some trees, so it looks as if a few leaves are sprouting from her head.

The graduation photograph, 1958

Three years after her death, I took this photograph to the Dharamshala house, placing it beside the other family photographs on the covered tin trunk. I wanted to retrieve the mother I knew. All the years that I lived with my mother, education was at the centre of our lives – hers and mine. There was never the slightest doubt in my mind that the excellence we were striving for was excellence in learning.

For a long time, the main story I told myself about my mother was about a woman who had struggled hard to educate herself. She used Partition as a liberating force. During the many years when Mummy worked to complete her Master's degree, her friends at university and some in the family would tell me, "Your mother has a lot of *himmat*" – courage, energy and daring. But that was the only mother I knew and I did not regard it as unusual.

My mother had completed the 8th class when her father insisted that she leave school. A series of small, determined steps – assisted by the upheaval of traditional norms and opportunities because of Partition – had her standing under the trees with her Master's degree in hand. For me this was the epic story of her life. I saw in her story an Indian woman's fight for independence.

But parallel to the story of my mother's education was another story. At her graduation ceremony at the University of Delhi in 1958, she was alone. By 1958, our family home had dissolved. My father had left home and was living at his clinic. My mother was living at the Working Girls' Hostel. I was in the hostel at Queen Mary's School in Delhi. Lata and Ranjan were already married and living in Bombay and New York respectively. But for us in Delhi, the traditional structures had fallen away.

The search for education

My mother sneaked in a BA (Hons) in Punjabi during the time when my father was posted to Iraq for one-and-a-half years during the Second World War. In the early 1940s in Punjab, it was possible to do the BA (Hons) known as *Gyani* as a single subject without having a general BA or even a Matriculation. Another young woman in the neighbourhood, whose husband had also gone to war, was preparing for the Punjabi BA (Hons) exam. The tuition classes were for three hours a day at the Gurdwara. My mother went along to see whether she could also do it. The tutor asked her to write an essay on God, and Mummy was able to draw on her knowledge of the scriptures and write a five-page essay. She was in.

Bauji was staying with Mummy, Lata and Ranjan while Pitajee was away. My mother upbraided him for not allowing her to continue her education, whereas the bride he chose for his son Khojinder had a BA. Bauji remonstrated that in those days that was the custom, but gave her tacit permission to study. My mother did not write to Pitajee, thinking he would stop her if he could, even though he was in Iraq.

After completing the Gyani, Mummy enrolled to study English at the Government College, Rawalpindi. But Pitajee came back earlier than expected and brought the study to a halt. Sewing classes, embroidery classes – these were acceptable. University education was not. "He did not like it", Mummy said. "But he couldn't do anything about my having passed the Gyani. He couldn't have me failed, could he?"

It was this BA (Hons) in Punjabi that launched my mother into an educational career in Delhi. Ranjan had studied Punjabi and needed to continue to study the language in her last years at school. But Miss Devi Dutta, the principal of Queen Mary's School where Ranjan was enrolled, said, "We do not have a Punjabi teacher." To this Mummy said, "I have done Punjabi Honours. I can teach my daughter Punjabi at home."

Miss Devi Dutta countered, "We have the princesses of Patiala who tell us every day that they want to study Punjabi. So why don't you teach Punjabi in our school? We'll give you an honorarium." At first my mother received Rs 50 a month. To that was added another Rs 30 to make up Rs 80. My mother says:

I did not see it as my money. It was the respect I got there – I used to feel proud of that. I remember that Devi Dutta respected me a lot. My colleagues gave me a lot of respect. Students who were princesses used to bring chairs for me. In a way it was as if they were grateful to me. I felt that I knew something, I could teach somebody something. At home, Pitajee used to only get angry at me. I got a bit of confidence in my own personality.

This money was helpful but not crucial to the family finances. My father's clinic at the time was the only one in the neighbourhood and he was making Rs 200, Rs 250 a month. Mummy said, "At that time your Pitajee did not say anything. Later, he would say, 'She teaches for Rs 50.'"

My mother was successful as a teacher. Ranjan got a distinction in her Punjabi and all the other students did well. My mother was proud of her record as a teacher and would say, "Our results were cent per cent."

Now that she was teaching students who were completing their Year 10, the principal, Miss Devi Dutta, suggested that she ought to complete Year 10 herself. This was towards the end of 1948. By this time we had moved from Mama Jaidev Singh's house to Mama Amarjeet's house in Sujan Singh Park. A child in the neighbourhood used to get tuition for his Year 10 exam. My mother persuaded Pitajee to allow her to get a month's tuition and appear for the Year 10 exam. After two months' study she passed her Year 10 exam.

By this time, however, she had already begun tutoring students studying Punjabi at the BA level at Miranda House, University of Delhi. One of Mama Amarjit's friends had a daughter who was weak in Punjabi. My mother started tutoring her. The girl told the Principal, Miss V. Thakurdas, about Mummy and how satisfied she was with the lessons. Miss Thakurdas asked to meet my mother as she had been looking for a Punjabi teacher.

When Mummy went to see Miss Thakurdas at home, she was washing her hair. While she was washing her hair, she asked Mummy questions and talked to her in Punjabi. Soon after, my mother started teaching Miranda House girls Punjabi on a semi-private basis, with each girl paying Rs 10 a month. There were 20 or 25 girls, so Mummy would bring home Rs 200 to Rs 250 a month.

This time around, the money was needed at home, for Pitajee's practice had dwindled. He only had a couple of patients a day. Lata had also begun working at the Refugee Handicrafts, the precursor to the Cottage Industries Emporium, and was earning Rs 150 a month.

My mother taught at Miranda House for nine years. She would go four days a week to Miranda House and two days a week to Queen Mary's. In the evenings, for many years, she taught at a private college, Kurukshetra College. The college was about five miles away and it meant going by bicycle, but it was worth another Rs 100 a month.

In a near repeat of what had happened at Queen Mary's School, Miss Thakurdas, who became a friend, told Mummy, "Mrs Singh, you teach BA students. At the very least, you should do your BA." So my mother started the long haul to obtain a full-fledged BA. In the 1950s, one could do it in a two-step process: the FA first, followed by a BA, subject by subject. Pitajee was angry about her doing her FA. He said, "Passing the Matric is one thing. Passing the FA is totally another." But with the extra income from the evening classes, she was able to get a month's private tuition for Rs 125.

She did not pass. It was a two-year course, and a month's tuition was not enough. She finally passed her FA in 1950 but failed the BA English subject twice. She says:

Every time I failed I was sad. Pitajee used to say, "Dullard. Dullard." I could only study after 9 p.m. for two hours. Each time I failed, he would say, "She has failed again. She can't pass." Then I would say, "I will show him by passing."

I used to have a cousin who would say the old and decrepit can't study. [Mummy was 40.] I told him this old and decrepit person will study. Well, I failed English. Next day I picked up the books again. Changed the tuition centre. Went to Gole Market, three miles further – 12 miles cycling, coming and going in the evening.

After passing her English exam in 1952, she began studying for her BA history exam at Kurukshetra College in the evening. I remember going with her sometimes on the back of her bicycle. She would sit among the students for one hour studying history and would then stand up to teach Punjabi for the second hour. A couple of her students would cycle back with her on dark winter nights and escort her home before going on to their homes. She would get back at night and her food would have been kept for her, but it was cold. I remember she was often desperately behind, and when I was eight, I would read British constitutional history to her while she was having dinner.

My mother failed the BA history the first time she appeared. Her command of English was always the stumbling point. She lacked fluency and confidence in English. She passed the second time around. So with English, History and the Punjabi she had already done, she completed a full BA in 1955.

For Mummy, the BA was an important milestone. But she says that for Pitajee it was difficult.

All the time I was away. Till I started on the BA, happy or sad, your Pitajee tolerated it. BA full was in 1955. In 1948, Matric, 1950 FA, 1952 BA English. I did not fail once a year, I would fail every six months. Every time I would send my admission in September and April.

An evening of adventure

For my mother this was a hard, though exciting time. I remember only the excitement it brought into my life. My only experience of drama as a child was going to Miranda House to see my mother's students enact tragic love stories such as *Sassi Punnu*. Or hearing Mummy and her students sing *Heer Ranjha*, also a story of doomed love.

My mother's life seemed to be full of adventures. The story I liked best was the one about Mummy saving a girl's honour when she was cycling back with her students from Kurukshetra College at about 8.30 one night. Near the bungalows at Shahjahan Road, a young girl was standing, surrounded by a large crowd of people and one or two policeman. My mother dismounted from her cycle and moved the people aside and asked the girl, "Where are you from?"

The girl was very beautiful. She had a broad face, a fair complexion. She was wearing jewellery and shimmering clothes. She said, "I am lost. Yesterday I got married. Today my in-laws took me to Hanuman temple. When we came out, I went one way and they went another way." She had been walking and walking. She dared not get into a taxi.

Just then, the wife of a noted cloth tycoon happened to pass by in a car. She stopped to check out the unusual situation. There was a newly married woman. There was my mother who was tall and strong. The cycles were also there. The tycoon's wife said, "I will send the car back for you. Please see her home." Her car came back. My mother sent her cycle with one of the boys. The other boy rode in the car with them with his cycle at the back.

However, first the policemen took them all to the police station. After the report had been made, the policemen said they would see the girl home the following day. Mummy insisted that the girl be allowed to go with her. She told the policemen that her uncle, Mama Atma Singh, was a member of parliament. Upon hearing this, they began to mollify her. My mother insisted that she would accompany the girl to her parents' home. She told the policemen, "You know if this girl stays even one night here, her honour will be lost. I am not saying you are bad, but it is the public view that any girl who has spent a night at the police station is not worth anything any more."

Two policemen accompanied my mother and the girl in the car. The student and his cycle went too. Mummy's voice lowers as she retells the story:

> When we went to her parents' house, there were a hundred people sitting there in a small house. When they saw us, they were mad with joy. They started shouting, "The girl has been found. The girl has been found." The in-laws were there too. I told them, "I have come with this girl to tell you personally that nobody has touched her. This girl is as untouched and pure as she was before. Now please look after your girl."

They began to prostrate themselves at my mother's feet, calling her, "Goddess, Goddess". Even the girl said, "For me the goddess appeared. For me a goddess appeared." My mother was very satisfied that she had been able to do a good deed. She came back home to find everybody was asleep. There was no food or water left for her. My mother says, "I went to sleep too. The next morning I told him I came home after midnight, and he was angry and said, 'Why take an unnecessary risk?'"

The bitter-sweet joy of MA in Punjabi literature

My mother began attending MA classes at the University soon after she completed her "full" BA in 1955. She would teach 12 students in the mornings at Miranda House – that brought in about Rs 150 – and then walk across to the university classes which started at about 10.30.

The Master's was a joy compared to the BA. My mother was now on solid ground for she no longer had to struggle with poor English. Her knowledge of the scriptures became a big asset as she was studying classical devotional poetry. The emphasis now was on getting a first division, something that had eluded her all her life. After studying for two years, in the preparatory holidays before the final exam, she developed a severe pain in her right arm and had to defer taking the exam. By that time, the marriage had disintegrated and my father had left home.

Ranjan says the trouble had begun when Mummy decided to take the first tuition at Miranda House. "Lata, Aijee and I had a long discussion before Aijee took the first tuition in 1948. We were against it because we thought Pitajee wouldn't be able to take it." But my father's earnings had begun to slip. He was a good, even brilliant, diagnostician but patients found his rough manner disconcerting. Some days he used to have only one or two patients the entire day. My mother said she had no choice but to go out and earn some money. Unlike their life in Rawalpindi, there was no grandmother here who would pay for the housekeeping or familiar traders with whom they could run up credit. The military life too was finished.

Lata was completing her BA, Ranjan was in Year 10 and I had not gone to school as yet. Mummy thought, how long can one depend on relatives? She said:

Life ahead looked very dark. Only Swaran was my support. Swaran would never let me be hard up. He would sign a cheque and leave it with me. In between, he would give me money. But in the life ahead, only I could do something. I had energy, enthusiasm and intelligence. Only if I stood up would I be able to look after my children. Pitajee could not do it.

Ranjan says:

Once she started giving tuitions, she wasn't asking Pitajee's permission whether she could go to another college. Then she started studying in order to teach. The result was that not only was she earning more money, but she also was not there.

Pitajee would come home and eat his meal alone, spend the afternoon alone, spend the evening alone. We were busy with our colleges. Pitajee was lonely. So when she came home, Pitajee had no sympathy for her. He had his own problems.

But money continued to be needed. I remember my father saying, "Why do the girls need to be educated? We can exist on salted *gram*." Lata had gone to Bombay to work with the Railways. Ranjan went to the hostel to complete her BSc at Lady Irwin College and then left for the United States on an exchange scholarship to Sarah Lawrence College. The fare to the United States was paid by loans and grants. Ranjan remembers my parents as still being a unit at the time. I don't remember them as such. For me, my mother was the one who paid my school fees, took me out, talked to me. My father was a figure looming sternly in the background.

For my father, life fell apart after Partition. Mummy changed as the times changed. But my father stayed still. He was no longer the breadwinner. Mummy's income kept increasing, his income kept decreasing. Mummy wanted kindness. Pitajee wanted obedience and recognition that he was the husband, the lord and master. But now his word was no longer unchallenged. For Pitajee, his years in the army were the brightest portion of his life. He talked continually of what the commanding officer had said to him. But everybody else had moved on. His world was slipping.

Ranjan remembers that the household was still there but cracking when we were in Lodhi Estate. My father could see his authority waning. Ranjan was invited to go to a seminar in Mysore. Pitajee objected saying some *lafangai* (irresponsible people) had organised it. Ranjan turned to him and said, "You don't even know who they are. How can you say that?"

Unable to take this questioning of his opinion, Pitajee left the house. Mummy followed him. Later Mummy said that Pitajee had cried because nobody listened to him any more. Afterwards he told Ranjan, "You two have already decided. All you want is a rubber stamp from me."

The fights between my mother and father increased. For a short time, at weekends, the three of us would play cut throat, a three-handed version of bridge, in the bedroom. My mother would bluff outrageously and often win. My father would get angry that she had not followed the rules, she had not played it right, and she still won. One day he said he was going to play no more. Thus the only kind of activity we enjoyed together stopped. There was no longer any laughter at home.

Chapter 9

Moving again

———

I have been living for 18 years in my house in Melbourne, surrounded by eucalyptus trees, wattles and hawthorn. Speaking of it one day, I realised that this is the longest I have ever lived in one house anywhere, whether in India, Malaysia or Australia.

I don't remember any of the things my mother and sisters recount about Karachi or Bombay. The first snatches of a scene I remember is sitting in the winter sun outside Mama Jaidev Singh's place in Delhi. My mother was braiding my hair in fine plaits in the style of her grandmother and then braiding the plaits into two thicker plaits.

My first clear memory is of the Ambassador Hotel. I must have been four-and-a-half when we lived there. We had two rooms on either side of the hall. We also had the use of the large terrace along which the name of the hotel now stands. I spent most of my time in the kitchen next door with the neighbours where Bhabhi (sister-in-law) lived. She was from Mussoorie and the only daughter-in-law in the family. She was young and pretty and loving. I remember squatting on the low wooden seat, seeing her peel the skin off the pea pods, while her mother-in-law cooked on the coal stove. Her husband was with the *Hindustan Times*. When there was a fire at Presentation Convent, my school during the kindergarten years, I felt very important for I could tell him the news. The youngest son of the house would take me around on the front of his cycle and do other odd chores for my mother. We kept in touch for a couple of years.

Below us lived a young married couple. Their only claim to fame was that the woman would call her husband "Darling Ji, Darling Ji", at a time when most women did not call their husbands anything at all, other than "Ei Ji. Oh Ji". So when we ran past her rooms, we would all shout, "Darling Ji, Darling Ji". In another part of the hotel lived Rani's parents with numerous children. My aunt Mami Bir,

Mama Swaran's wife, is Rani's cousin.

Much of the time Rani and her sisters and I played on the terrace together. We played doctor-doctor, making medicines out of sweets and flowers. Rani and her sisters were in a larger gang and they generally got to drink the sweet medicine. Looking back, I see this as a happy time, most of my memories revolving around food. I remember when Prem Singh, my childhood servant from Meerut, came by to tell us he had had a son. To celebrate, he took me to the shanty shops near Pitajee's clinic and bought me a cream roll. It was pastry with cream spilling out of it – an unusual treat. And once, my father took me to the shop at the side of the Ambassador Hotel to teach me that one anna was made up of four pice. He gave me an anna and I bought four sugar-coated almonds, white, blue and pink, because each of them cost one paisa.

I caught the mumps and that was also a celebratory time. My main concern was that we should quickly telephone Lata so that she could bring me a basket of fruit. I was worried that the fever might not last and then I would not get any fruit. And who knew when I would fall ill again. I also remember Ranjan having a Western-style birthday party on the terrace – the first and last party that I remember in our house. Her friends played musical chairs and she had balloons. And they let me play.

I don't remember any toys. I became conscious of that only when my son Sunil bought me a University teddy bear to mark my PhD graduation. But it was not a gap that I particularly felt in my life. My world in those years was populated by family and neighbours. Mama Khojinder and his family used to live in a tent not too far away. Mama Swaran would come by with his friends. One day there was a car honkng below our place. We looked out and there was Mama Swaran with his first car, a brown and cream Vauxhall.

I always waited for him to come and visit from the Air Force mess. Knowing that my mother would cook up a storm for him, I hoped he would want to eat her wonderful roast mutton and rice pudding. "No, no", he would tell his sister, "make me lentils, *mahn ki dal*, sister. And make me cauliflower and crumple up the bread the way Baiji used to do." There was a lot of laughter and joy when he came. But no mutton or rice pudding.

Mummy builds a house in Nizamuddin

During the school and university holidays in 1952, while she was teaching in three places and studying for her BA, my mother built our house in Nizamuddin. We had received the land as compensation for the house we had lost in Rawalpindi. She had it completed during the summer holidays in two-and-a-half months. Pitajee was angry about the house. He saw no need for it and thought it would be better to cash in the claim, but Mummy persisted. She had never built a house. She turned to her cousin, Harkishen, the son of Mama Jaidev Singh. He was having his house constructed so he had the architect draw up a plan to her design.

Mummy had to go and stand in the sun to supervise the construction of the house. Uncle Harkishen would come to the site every day. It was a time of cement rationing. She went to Mama Amarjit, with whom we had stayed in Sujan Singh Park. He worked with a cement company. Mummy needed 200 bags of cement. He said, "I am sorry I can't give you 200 bags. But I can give you a wagon load of 500. You can dispose of the other 300, and if you make a profit I will be pleased. But you have to pay me for 500."

My mother had started out with Rs 6000 in the account. This had come partly from the compensation for property lost during Partition. But the money soon ran out. Mama Swaran came to the rescue. He down-plays it, saying, "I had a little money and I gave it to her." Uncle Harkishen also gave her Rs 2000.

Pitajee remained antagonistic and unconvinced. He did not visit the building site even when the roof went up. When Mummy collapsed in the heat, Lata went to supervise the construction for five days. Lata says:

What made it worse was that Chacha Sanmukh came and both brothers started talking. Aijee was wanting to put chips in ordinary cement so that there would be colour. These two said, "Now you will want to put colour also." All the time they would sit and talk.

I told Aijee to forget about him. If you want to build the house, then you do it. One day Aijee came home at 2.30 and she wanted her lunch. But Pitajee was the doctor sahib. He said, "This is no time to have lunch." I told Aijee, "You eat. Let me see how you can't eat." I told him, "This is our house just as much as it is your house."

When the house was complete, we stayed there for a while before the tenants moved in. The pump brought up potable sweet water and a shout went up, "The water is sweet, the water is sweet." There was no electricity and we used hurricane lamps. There were also oil lamps with glass chimneys that had to be cleaned every evening. I was already enrolled in Presentation Convent and my bus would arrive on dark winter mornings. My sisters had the duty of doing my hair on such mornings. I did not want Lata to do my hair as it would come undone and I would get a black mark. But soon, Lata left for Bombay to work.

I was sent off to the Mussoorie hills to stay for nine-month stretches in a residential school for, like my mother, I was sensitive to the heat. Lata funded my two-year stay in the school hostel, which was run by the Railways. The best bits were nature walks and the library. The food was terrible. Mummy had said I should be a vegetarian, for she was not sure whether they would give me *jhatka* meat (the meat that had been ritually slaughtered in the Sikh way with one stroke of the sword). But vegetarian food meant pumpkin every day. When I came home, I gained weight on the lentils that were cooked at home.

Lodhi Estate

Money remained tight during the 1950s. We rented out the Nizamuddin house and in turn rented one bedroom, a bathroom and a verandah in Lodhi Estate, near the Lodhi Gardens. It was part of a bungalow which was the official accommodation given to a Lieutenant Colonel we knew. The kitchen was a tent down a pathway.

In the one bedroom, Mummy, Pitajee, Ranjan and I slept. I guess if any guests came, they slept on the verandah. This had been converted into a living room. Bamboo *chics* lined with navy blue cloth used to come down at night.

The verandah looked out on the side garden. There was a mulberry tree and a hedge of verbena with bluish black berries that you could eat. To the right of the kitchen tent was the vegetable garden of the main house. I don't remember the front garden, for it was out of bounds. I knew there were cannas in the summer. Actually, the whole garden was prohibited territory, for the Colonel's wife did not like my taking any flowers for the house. She did not mind when I took only the leaves.

We had a servant from the hills. He would go home once a year for a month to visit his wife who worked the land. He must have slept in the tent or on the verandah. Though money in the house must have been tight, I never thought about it. There was always a rupee to give to the woman who came to massage my mother, always money to give for *shagan,* the ritual gifts at births and marriages. "What does it matter? What does it matter?" Mummy would say. "Your mind should be full." So it did not matter that the clothes were hand-me-downs, for wasn't it true that I went to the best schools and did well in my studies?

My mother would weave dreams of what we would do and where we would go. Every now and again my father would puncture this dreaming and say, "Stop this tomfoolery." My mother would laugh and say, "We are only making our hearts feel glad."

Most often food meant lentils – lots of them – raw onion, pickles and mint chutney, with hot puffed-up *phulkas*. The drinking water would be kept in round clay pots (*gharas*) which kept the water cool and imparted the smell of earth to it. I don't think ours were the new-fangled ones with taps on the side. We had to take the water out with a long-handled scoop. I have a clay pot like that in my kitchen in Dharamshala.

The kitchen had an *angithi*, a stove made from a tin bucket lined with mud, with three mounds on the top for the pots. The *angithi* would be lit in the morning – a layer of the stone coal that stayed hot all day long, with a bit of the more expensive wood coal to start the fire going. My mother and I bought this coal from a large coal shed, where the different kinds of coal lay in separate heaps.

The servant would make the *chapatis* on the iron griddle, remove the griddle from the stove with tongs, then place a *chapati* directly on the coals and wait for it to puff up. Before running with it to the living room, he would place another *chapati* on the griddle. The only time I thought about it at all was when Mummy and Pitajee had an argument. Pitajee was angry that the *chapati* wasn't puffed up, that it had deflated. Mummy was saying, "Don't shout so. It is very cold and the servant is doing the best he can."

Pickles were an important part of the meal. My mother would make the mango pickle in the summer and the cauliflower, carrot and turnip pickles in the winter. In the winter too, she would make *kanji,* a spicy drink made from deep red carrots in a large earthen pot. And in between there was the lime pickle with ginger and green chillies.

The important ritual occasion was making the summer mango pickle. When the mangoes were cheap, my mother bought 20 seers (roughly 40 kg) of raw mangoes. She borrowed a special scythe and sat in the sun on the lawn outside, cutting each mango into eight pieces – each piece had to have its own bit of the seed and stone. The servant would have washed the many spices – I particularly remember the fennel and rye – and they would be out in the sun to dry.

I was relegated to the fringes of this activity. "Don't touch. Don't touch", my mother warned. If a drop of water touched the pickle, it would not keep and we would not have pickles for the rest of the year. There were also other unknowns. It was well known that my mother's hands were good with pickles, for her pickles lasted for years.

Ranjan moved to the Lady Irwin College hostel to prepare for her BSc exams as there was no place to study at home. My mother took on extra tuition in the afternoon to pay for it. Ranjan did brilliantly, sweeping nearly all the prizes, and soon left for New York on a scholarship to Sarah Lawrence College. The prizes came after she left, so I spent my evenings and holidays reading her books, particularly Oscar Wilde. I was nine.

I remember being alone most of the time. Some weekends, we would go to Mama Khojinder's place and I would play, or most often fight, with my cousins. Mama Khojinder used to have a car he loved, an old car that he had to crank up. And that also did not always work. So most of the time, we had to push it to get it to start. They would visit us at home sometimes, and Manjit (Babbar), Gurmit (Cheeta) and I would go outside the house and shake the tamarind tree, eating raw tamarind till our teeth were on edge. The only other time I have had raw tamarind was on the beach in Arnhem Land in Australia.

Masi Gyaan's children (Bapuji's grandchildren) would also come to our place and we fought with each other. Now Bindi and I see that as a bond.

The three children in the Colonel's home were kept cordoned off by their mother. They were always trying to escape her for she continually pestered them to study. For the most part, I would hang around the edges of the garden, watching their mother move the flow of water from one vegetable bed to another. She would break the ridges between the beds if she wanted the water to flow and build them up again if she wanted to keep the water out.

Men would be working in the garden or around the area. They would see a nine-year-old child by herself. Their attempts to fondle me were interrupted by the servant coming in or somebody in the main house coming outside. But the shopkeeper in a shop not too far from my father's would have me sit on his lap and masturbate me.

The main event after school was that once a week the servant would take me on the bicycle to the library of the Education Department. My father's cousin, Kirna, had made it possible for me to borrow books. That year I read Enid Blyton and Andrew Lang. I remember telling my father that I would never read anything but Enid Blyton and he did not laugh.

Khyber Pass

When I was 11 we moved again. Now that I am counting, this was the ninth move after Meerut, Karachi, Bombay and five places in Delhi. This time we moved to Khyber Pass in Old Delhi to live in part of Nanaji's estate. The rent was Rs 50 a month. It was cheap, for Nanaji's grandson Zorawar, my mother's first cousin, was in charge. Its other attraction was that it was close to Delhi University where Mummy was now studying for her MA. I moved to Queen Mary's School in Tis Hazari, where Ranjan had studied and where my mother had taught.

Uncle Sharan's family – the same Sharan who had been in Karachi – lived in the buildings to one side. There was another distant uncle – I called him father's younger brother – staying in the other part of the first-floor apartment. They had a black labrador.

Below us at the front were shops selling flour, groceries, fruit. Just below us was a young bride who would weave cotton *durries* on her loom. This loom filled nearly the whole room in her house. I would often sit outside her front step seeing her weave. More than 45 years later, the memory of her weaving inspired the exhibition I initiated about Punjabi *durrees* and *baghs* at the Immigration Museum in Melbourne.

Just opposite the house was a well, shaded by a tree. It was a functioning well where travellers stopped. There was also a travellers' rest place with water in earthen pots, a rich man's service to the community to lay up merit for his next life. And beyond the road to the front and to the right of us was the ridge, a dry forest area with the thin-leafed *kikar* (acacia nilotica) trees. Under these trees, deeper in the forest, mushrooms grew. Further away, but still within walking distance, was the Jamuna river.

We usually had visitors staying with us. My father's eldest sister's husband came to stay because he wanted to see the International Exhibition. He would be out all day but in the evening he provided much amusement. He was known to be simple and my mother teased him mercilessly. One day, he was sitting on the commode but had forgotten to latch the door. Mummy opened the door by mistake and, when she saw him there, she said, "Bhaiajee (sister's husband), why don't you sell tickets for the show?" The humour in the house was definitely anal. Once my mother farted at the dining table but everybody, including Mummy, looked at Bhaiajee, assuming he was the culprit. And Bhaiajee said, "Well, I suppose it must have been me." Pitajee once told Mummy to cool it, that perhaps it was not seemly to pull his leg all the time. Mummy quietened down. Bhaiajee said he was leaving. There was no fun in the home any more. So the teasing started again.

Bapuji and Professor Thakur Singh would also come to visit. If they came in the winter, they brought pickles made of spinach stems. In the summer, they brought roasted cornflour which we mixed with sugar or molasses and water and drank to chase away the heat.

Parties at home meant that Mama Khojinder and Mama Harbans (Bapuji's son) and their families came to visit. On special occasions like birthdays, we bought *gulab jamuns*. It was not till I went to university that I discovered that parties could include non-kin.

The house we stayed in had been elegant in former times when Delhi's administrative district was in Civil Lines. Now it was decrepit. Our part of the house had a large hall with wooden floors, what used to be the ballroom, and a bedroom for my parents, a prayer room and a bedroom for me. I never slept in my room. Most likely visitors stayed there. In that room, we also kept the beautiful rolltop desk that Masi Deep, my mother's cousin, had sent over from her house. At the same time she had sent two bone-handled knives, which became our kitchen knives. The third room also contained our clothes and I had a few books. Lata had sent me a book with a picture of Cinderella under a pink blossom tree, after her godmother had transformed her.

I don't remember the other furniture. Only the dressing table with the swivel mirror that my mother's grandmother had bought her in Murree moved with us when we left Pakistan. The wooden chest and tin trunk must have been there but I don't remember them. There was a dining table and there must have been a variety of chairs. There were old-fashioned *nawar* beds that we had to tighten by pulling the warp and weft. I surprised my neighbours in Dharamshala by weaving a chair with *nawar* and realised I had not forgotten the art of *nawar* weaving.

The kitchen was a hole in the wall, with just enough space for a bench on which the stove was placed. At that time, we did not have gas or a fridge. Back to back with the kitchen was a bathroom with commodes that the cleaning woman emptied every day and a bucket and mug to bathe with. In the summer we slept on the roof. You needed to know which stairs to jump over, because some had disintegrated. It was a game I played with my school friends when they came to visit. When the glass broke in the windows we replaced it with cardboard. In the prayer room, one night, the roof fell in. The ceiling – a kind of white parchment – held for a while, but in the end it too came tumbling down.

This was our last family home.

Chapter 10

My father's story

———

A rope bed was in the middle of the living room. My mother had gone to find my father at his clinic, an hour away by bus. She came back by bus, alone, so it must have been before midnight.

Uncle Sharan's family was clustered around, including his brother who used to try to expose himself to me when I was alone at home. The servant was there. It wasn't Prem Singh, who used to look after me as a child, for Mummy called him many days later after people started throwing stones through the windows. It must have been the one who used to go into fits in the square at the back.

Everyone was waiting, for a drama was unfolding. My mother came back alone. I don't remember any more of that night. I must have gone to sleep, but the memory is one of emptiness. I was 12.

My father leaves home

On 28 September 1955, Lata married Nandy in Bombay. Nandy was my mother's first cousin. His father and my mother's father were brothers. The marriage was performed without the presence of family, after a seven-year courtship in Bombay. Though marrying a maternal uncle is a preferred match in many parts of South India, in Punjab it infringed the traditional code of not marrying within five generations on your mother's side and seven generations on your father's side.

We received the news by telegram and did not tell anybody until we had confirmed that the telegram was genuine. Mummy sent me down to the shops to get some fruit to celebrate on the quiet. I think I got some *phalsai*, the tart, purplish black fruit one ate with salt and chillies.

In early 1956, Lata and Nandy came to Delhi after their first visit to Nandy's mother in Ludhiana. They came to the Khyber Pass house where we were staying. A day before they arrived, a letter came from Ranjan addressed to Lata. It had been redirected from Lata's office. My father opened it. His action was true to his belief that the emphasis on privacy within the family was a silly Western trait.

In the letter, Ranjan had written of her plans to marry Siva. She had mentioned Siva to us in her letters. I had even kidded her, asking whether Siva was her boyfriend. For my father, this was a bombshell. Siva was not a Sikh. It did not matter that he came from a well-known family in Kerala, that he was well educated, that he worked with the United Nations, that they loved each other. What was important to my father was that he was not a Sikh. My father had railed loud and long against parents who corrupted the religion by condoning inter-faith marriages. Now it had happened to him.

Lata and Nandy arrived, and somehow the reception that had been planned for them at home took place. After they left, nights of haranguing followed. I remember hysterical conversations between my parents – I usually slept between them – with my father brow-beating my mother to swear that her daughter was dead. He shouted and railed. My mother cried and talked of jumping into the well outside the house.

When my father did not return home, we suspected he had gone to see Bapuji in Tarn Taran, for the shopkeeper next door had heard my father asking for the time of the Amritsar train.

After that follows a blank period. Lata says she received a letter from Mummy in Bombay saying Pitajee had left home and she came to be with us. I do not remember that. When I was trying to piece together the story, I discovered that my father had indeed gone to Amritsar, to my mother's aunt's (Baiji's sister) house. They called us and so we knew where he was. From there he went to Ferozepur, where his uncle, his mother's brother, lived. Ranjan says that Pitajee also went to Dehradun to meet Bhai Vir Singh, the famous Punjabi poet and a friend of his maternal uncle, the poet Puran Singh. He was not allowed in by Bhai Vir Singh's minders and came back to Delhi.

My father returned to Delhi and moved into his clinic to live. He did not meet Ranjan and Siva for eight years. Mummy and I stayed for a few months in the house, huddled together. It was the two of us against the world. That idea did not fade. The nights were peopled with terror as my mother felt the menace of lecherous men around us. She called Prem Singh to come and stay with us at night.

Mama Swaran was in Delhi and he and Mummy went to plead with my father to come back. He refused.

It was 1956 and Mummy was 45. Expenses mounted. Mummy was still studying for her MA. The tenant in the Nizamuddin house wasn't paying his rent because he had gone bankrupt. So the only money coming in was from Mummy's teaching at Miranda House and some money that Ranjan and Lata sent. Food was often bought on credit. Sometimes for lunch the only dish was a curd curry – you could make it really tasty with a lot of ginger and chillies. If any of my friends from Queen Mary's came home with me, they thought it was special.

My father had left but he did not earn enough to support himself. Mummy had to initially supplement his living expenses at the clinic. She put me into Queen Mary's School hostel, after she had asked Miss Devi Dutta to ensure that nobody shamed me if the fees were sometimes late. She herself moved into a shared room in the Working Girls' Hostel on Curzon Road.

My mother's 28-year marriage was over. Most people thought it was my mother who had left her husband to study and live her own life. There was much sympathy for him. Often people would tell my mother, "Poor man, poor man. All alone." It never failed to upset her. She was the one who was seen to be at fault for she could not keep her man and her marriage. I heard her cousin throwing it at her at a wedding. We left, my mother in tears.

A failed marriage, a husband who had left home, was such a disaster that the fact that I had lost a home and a father was never discussed. It was not something I myself talked about fully for over 40 years.

A life alone

For my father, it meant a life with no home comforts. He would drag the narrow consulting couch – just over two feet wide and made of woven cane – to the front part of the shop and sleep there. He had to move his chair aside and the couch would then be by his table with the green iron cash box at its foot. He would arch his stiff back and pull the iron shutters down with difficulty. The clinic would become a bedroom with medicine cupboards all around.

There was no toilet in the clinic at first, so he would use the smelly communal toilets in the back lane. He would bathe inside the clinic. For food, he would go to the rough food shop at the other end of the road. He would have his usual two *chapatis* but the vegetables were too spicy. His clothes were in a small tin trunk – four or five white *kurtas* and pyjamas, along with an envelope of pornographic pictures that he must have received by mail. His black coat hung from a hanger on a nail in the alcove behind the dispensary.

In time, when rent started coming in from the house again, he had a toilet made at the back, and installed a gas stove and a small fridge. Then he would make *chapatis* for himself and stock cokes in the fridge for visitors. The consulting couch was replaced by a sofa which is now in Ranjan's place in Delhi.

He remained in the clinic until he retired. At any rate, he was there until 1972 when I visited India with my sons, Aman and Sunil. When he retired, his clinic was rented out and he lived for the rest of his life in the home in Nizamuddin that my mother built.

Though the home had disintegrated, the family framework remained. My mother and I would visit my father at the clinic and eat in the shops with him. The expectations of filial behaviour remained the same. He too remained the same, expecting respect and obedience.

In 1965 I fell in love with an Indian from Trinidad who was studying history at Delhi University. True to form, my father stopped speaking to me. On his way back to Trinidad, the man wrote breaking off the relationship. I left for New Jersey to study on a scholarship. My father was still not speaking to me. After a few months, he wrote to me or perhaps to Ranjan in New York, saying he was now speaking to me again.

I came back to Delhi, began working at the Institute of Economic

Growth, got married to Charan and went to Malaysia to live. I wrote to my father when I had to. Whenever I came back to Delhi to visit, my mother or Lata would say, "Go see your father, you have been here two days; go see your father, it has been a week; go see your father." So I would go, taking him the silk handkerchiefs I had brought – he would use only silk – ask him whether he would like tea, pour tea, and never have one serious conversation with him. I had no questions about his life.

In a visit of two weeks, I would see him a couple of times, and only briefly. I remember once he could not stay away and came to see me at Lata's house. Once I gave him something I liked, an embroidered red bedcover from Rajasthan.

The charade of a filial relationship was maintained. I broke out of the filial charade only twice. I was 14 years old and in Queen Mary's School Hostel and fell ill with a high fever, high enough to be sent to the adjacent St Stephen's Hospital. When Miss Devi Dutta wanted to inform my father, I told her firmly not to bother. "Just tell my mother", I told her. "My father will not come."

The second time was when I was visiting Delhi with my sons, Aman and Sunil. They were nearly three and two. They would sit outside his clinic and were entranced by the horse-drawn wagons, the tongas, which would be loaded with tents and poles and chairs from the neighbour's shop. My father would give them as many Cokes as they wanted. Then he bought them two large boxes of chocolates and brought them to Lata's place where we were staying.

I erupted. I told him, "How dare you bring boxes of chocolates for my children when you never bought me a single chocolate, a single present?" He said something like "Churiai" which translates as "Sweeperess" and was his way of being affectionate. But I was totally without compassion. For me it brought back the days when we had lived together in the Lodhi Estate house and I wanted him to take me to the Red Fort because I had been ill and had missed the school outing. He wouldn't. In the end, my mother took me.

There were never any birthday presents from him, never any recognition of special days. I wrote to him for years from the Queen

Mary's School hostel every week, for we had a letter-writing period. He never wrote back. He did not come to visit, except towards the very end, when I was preparing for my higher secondary examinations. Then he would take me for a walk in the gardens in Old Delhi. Lata had told him he had to reciprocate. I went to university, debated, won prizes. He never came. Here he was playing grandfather without having been a father.

He didn't try to mend his fences with me. He told Lata I was too much my mother's daughter to want to hear his story. Even if he had spoken, most likely I would not have heard. I punished him and myself for walking out on me by making him count for nothing.

Pitajee did write to Mummy, 20 years after he had left home, telling her to let "bygones be bygones". She was by then the principal of a women's college in Patti, near Amritsar. But Mummy had waited 12 years in the Working Girls' Hostel in Delhi for him to say that. It was eight years too late for her and she did not reply.

Lata says:

Towards the end of his life he begged Aijee to come. She did not want to come. He wrote to her. He said, "Let's forget what happened in the past." He wrote to her again after Professor Thakur Singh died, for he thought maybe she was staying in Amritsar because of him.

When she came to Delhi, I told her. "I will arrange everything. There are two empty rooms in the Nizamuddin house. Stay there four or five days."

My mother did come back to Nizamuddin once to visit. She brought the girl who looked after her. But then Pitajee said something like, "Why do you roam around all day?" Mummy could not bear his attempt to reassert control. Mummy also told me that my father said to her one morning, "I had left my door open all night." My mother left soon after. She continued to visit him when she came to Delhi but never stayed.

My father's life was a life alone. He spent most of his day in the front room. The sofa bed had come from his clinic. There was a telephone on the side and a coffee table in front of the bed, where he would eat his meals. A radio was in the cupboard against one wall. I don't remember any photographs. There were a couple of chairs for guests. His medical books and medicine cupboards were in another room.

In the morning he would walk a mile or so to the Gurdwara. Later, he would also read from the Guru Granth Sahib in the prayer room. He had a servant at home cooking and cleaning for him. Lata used to visit regularly. Ranjan was in New York and I was in Malaysia. Half the office was rented out to an organisation, and my father and the clerk would have lunch together. His sister Tripat and her daughter came to see him. So did some of his cousins, the sons and daughters of his mother's brother. Masi Darshan would visit him and, depending on what was happening in her life, would sometimes stay.

My father died in his sleep in the Nizamuddin house in 1992 when he was 94. I was relieved that neither my mother nor my sisters suggested that I come for the final prayers. I remember upbraiding my mother when I heard her grieving on the telephone, saying she had no reason to pretend to me. But she herself was surprised at the intensity of her feelings at his death, at the loss of her husband.

I told myself that one day I would plant a lemon tree for him in Melbourne in the courtyard in front of the kitchen. I did not mourn him. Now that he was dead, I did not have to pretend filial respect any more. But it was not until my mother's death that the pain and anger spilled out.

"I haven't had time to think"

When I began writing this book, I asked myself how old my father would have been when he left home? I calculated he was 58. It shook me that in all these years I had never asked myself such a basic question. I was 53 at the time and could see retirement looming ahead and was planning for it. What could have induced a man to leave his wife and family, his home comforts, to live in his clinic? How had he felt? How did he cope?

He didn't talk about it. Rani, one of my father's patients who came from a family that had lived near us in Refugee Block – Mami Bir's cousin – remembers her mother saying, "Doctor Sahib, at this age, what have you done?" And this is what Doctor Sahib said, "By the grace of God, I haven't had time to think about it."

He did not talk about it even with his younger sister, Tripat. They never spoke about his leaving home, about his opposition to Ranjan's marriage. Five years after his death, when I sought out Bhua Tripat, she said, "When he moved to the clinic, he did not say anything and I did not say anything. I asked him how he had organised things. He would tell. We all ate, then he left. We did not want to touch on this topic. I did not ask."

She had her opinions that she stated clearly when I asked. She said, "Phappaji [big brother] troubled everybody a lot. All day, all night, Bhabhiji [sister-in-law] was looking for him. Go here, go there. Till midnight. He spoilt his whole life. He became alone."

They were not a talking family. My father would visit his sister every alternate weekend. Then too they would not discuss it. Bhuaji said, "He would come to sit, to laugh, and so why talk of things that hurt? I did not ask." She repeated, "What was the point of talking? We knew it all. Why keep returning to the same thing?"

His family was not demonstrative and they accepted Pitajee as he was. Bhuaji and her family would visit him regularly in the clinic and then later in Nizamuddin. If they did not visit in Nizamudin once a month, he would call saying, "What's happened? Are you planning to meet me in the next world?" Yet when Bhuaji was ill and in hospital with a stroke, he never went to visit. He never phoned. Bhuaji's daughter, Jatti, says:

We did not feel bad. We knew what kind of person he is. Lata said, "You love your sister, and you haven't asked after her even once." Who knows why? He was an interesting personality. Mama after her illness went to see him. He didn't say anything other than "You are all right now?"

Once, just once, he gave his sister a present. It was a toaster, the manual kind, where you had to turn the two slices of bread to toast them on both sides. Bhuaji and Jatti dwell on this memory as if stroking it. As they sit in their living room in Delhi, Jatti remembers also how he bought her some rouge from the Army Canteen in Meerut. And once, yes, they remember, he brought a box of sweets when he came to visit.

They did not mark the brother-sister relationship with the customory *rakhi* ritual when once a year, sisters tie coloured strings on their brothers' wrists to show their love and brothers give them money and gifts to signify that they will always be there for their sisters. Jatti also does not tie a *rakhi* on her brother. But Bhuaji told me how one weekend when he was visiting, she and her husband had an argument. Pitajee did not like Bhuaji's husband speaking loudly to Bhuaji. Bhuaji said, "It was natural. He was a brother."

When Pitajee died, his nieces and nephews all wanted something of his as mementos. But he had few possessions – some *kurtas* and pyjamas, sweaters, glasses and a circlet of iron prayer beads.

Bhuaji sobbed bitterly. She was in her 80s, but for her his death marked the end of her *paikai*, her natal kin. He was the only *paikai* she had ever had. In the days after Pitajee's death, Ranjan says Bhuaji said, "My brother died alone." Jatti said, "What do you expect when he brought it on himself?" Then Bhuaji noted that I had not come for the funeral. Ranjan said, "Kuki [my nickname at home] never forgave Pitajee for leaving home." Bhuaji said, "Neither did I."

Bhuaji

Bhuaji and I hardly had a relationship. I remembered fondly the few times I had visited her house when I was in college. I don't know why I went. I think it must have been my mother who told me to go. Bhuaji would welcome me and bring out her stores of salty and spicy snacks and set about making me something nice to eat. But there was little conversation and for me, at any rate, they represented my father's side of the family – not people I wanted to cultivate.

I started visiting her again after my father died. I had come to

Delhi to visit my mother before her gallbladder operation in 1993. Bhuaji came to call on my mother and saw me. She complained I had often come to Delhi and left without calling on her. I tried to pass it off, saying I was always ready to come for dinner.

But the point had been made – not visiting her had been a filial infringement. And she had cared enough to notice. So I began to call on them each time I went to Delhi and made sure I had dinner there. There was no real talk between us. If either of my sisters accompanied me, after asking me if I was well, the conversation drifted to the more familiar grooves of their life in Delhi or the rest of my father's family. But the relationship had been affirmed.

When I began wondering about my father's life as I began writing about my mother, I talked to Bhuaji and Jatti about two years before Bhuaji's death. The story that spilled out took me by surprise. The first surprise was the picture of my father as a loving man, a man who loved his family, a man who loved his wife. Jatti said:

> He loved Mamiji [my mother]. He talked about her with a lot of love. Papaji had a prostate operation and Pappu [her brother] and I and Mama went to get him in a taxi. He said, "Sorry, I can't go with you, for Inder is in hospital in Amritsar. A phone call may come." He was concerned, he was nervous. When she had her operation in Delhi, he was worried and nervous. He wasn't talking to anybody. He was saying his prayers.
>
> He never talked against her. If anybody tried to criticise her, he would snub the person. He wanted to live with her again.

The second surprise was the picture Bhuaji drew of a family abandoned after their mother died. I did not know much of my father's story, except that his mother had died when he was 17. He used to say that it was his mother who wanted him to be a doctor. She had wanted people to come knocking on the door for her son and asking, "Is Doctor Sahib in?"

His father, like Mummy's father, was a postmaster. Their mother's name was Lajwati but she was called Lajja. She was married so young that she had her first child at 14. She had stomach pains and died in her mid-30s. When she died, the eldest daughter was already married and expecting a child. Pitajee was 17 and soon to go to medical school in Lahore. Bhua Tripat was nine and the younger brothers, Appar and Sanmukh, were younger still.

But Pitajee's father, Teja Singh, unlike Mummy's father, never married again, fearing there would be too much trouble in the family. He was a harsh, undemonstrative father who came from a lineage of hard men. Jatti remembers her grandfather – mine also – as being so strict that she did not want to visit him in Sialkot. Unlike Mummy's story, the maternal and paternal kin did not step into the breach. The children were left to their own devices to wander the streets, uncared for, unkempt. The youngest, Sanmukh, had had polio and Bhuaji often had to carry him on her hip. "It was terrible", Bhuaji says, thinking back to that time.

The mother dies, the children's lives are ruined. All day we would roam around like vagrants. Shoes off, *salwar* coming off. Wander here, wander there, without any consciousness. There was nobody to stop us, nobody to tell us to study. Nobody to ask us if we had eaten.

She shudders and says that she does not want to think about that terrible time.

Their father would be away working all day. He had never looked after children. "He never understood what was happening", Bhuaji said. "He was hard. Quite hard." As a postmaster, he was transferred from place to place. When their mother died, they were at Daskai, near Sialkot. Sometimes the children went with him. Sometimes they went to stay with their maternal or paternal kin. Both sides were well off.

Their grandfather, Jai Singh, that is, my paternal great-grandfather, was a wine and liquor merchant in Sadar Bazar, Sialkot. He had a two-storey house in the city. I remember my father telling me about the family occupation of selling liquor. In the Indian caste system, this is not something to boast about, for selling liquor is a very low-caste occupation. But my father would stress that his grandfather never touched a drop.

My paternal grandmother ruled her own house in Sialkot. She was beautiful and with a lot of grace, but did not do much work even in her own house. She did not want to leave her house and come and look after her son's children. This is the paternal grandmother, the Dadiji who stayed the last years of her life with my mother and father. She was also the one who was given the bracelets that Nanaji had given my mother.

Their mother's family was well-to-do in Rawalpindi, the maternal grandfather being a surveyor. But the grandmother ruled in her own home. The children would stay sometimes with their maternal kin, sometimes with their paternal kin but, according to Bhuaji, they had no sense of home or place. The younger children grew up with virtually no education, though their maternal uncle Puran Singh became one of the esteemed poets and thinkers of his time.

Even when their father went to China to work, the traditional family supports failed them. It was suggested that the children go to Lahore so that my father could look after them while he was studying there. But that did not happen. I never heard my father speak of this. Bhuaji was placed in Khalsa School in Ferozepur. She did not want to talk of that time – little food, falling ill and being scared of the dark. She was 12. Later, the three children stayed mostly with their father's mother in Sialkot. Bhuaji remembers her as being strict.

Bhuaji was ill for many years. But then life took a more traditional turn when her father's friend virtually adopted her and arranged her marriage in 1922. As a result, she moved to Delhi. But the only *paikai* she had was my father and mother in Rawalpindi. That is where she would come with her children to visit.

I don't know exactly what happened to my father's younger brothers. For a while they worked with their father in the liquor shop where he worked after he had retired as postmaster. Their father died in Sialkot in 1936. Appar continued in the family tradition selling liquor in Bombay, particularly during Prohibition. The joke in the family was that Appar would go on a yearly pilgrimage to pray for the continuance of the Congress Party in power because that meant a continuation of Prohibition and an assurance his profits would continue. I saw Uncle Appar only a couple of times when he visited Lata in Bombay when I happened to be visiting too. His passion was Indian sweetmeats.

Sanmukh, the youngest, lived off his wits and gambling. He was a devotee of Hanuman, the Hindu monkey god. Sanmukh was said to be greatly admired for his magical powers. One story that did the rounds was that he had meditated so long in the Himalayas that one leg became shorter than the other. He is said to have cured some ruler's daughter of cancer and the ruler was forever grateful.

I did not know him well, for my father and he had had a major falling out when I was 10. Nobody really talked of it. But when I went to Bombay to stay with Lata during the summer vacations, I used to spend a day with him. Depending on his finances, we would either get take-away Chinese food or something simpler. He would look at me, a gawky teenager with acne, and try to make me look seductive by using some of his creams and lotions. On one visit, he said my eyes needed help, so he had his secretary/partner line my eyes with a particular concoction of kohl. I thought I did look seductive but my sister Lata saw me and asked, "Why are your eyes tearing?"

He was a striking presence – balding head, piercing eyes, long hair loose and a long black beard. He used to visit us in Lodhi Estate until the quarrel with my father and mother. He was known to give lavish presents but then remind you forever that he had given them.

Uncle Sanmukh bet on horses so he was either flush and we were having Chinese food all day long, or he was broke and all was lost. He had a companion, a Parsee woman, who was also his secretary. She had a twilight kind of presence – not quite accepted as his wife, except at the very end. Uncle Sanmukh came to my father's clinic when he knew he was dying. At his death, my parents called for his companion and she mourned him as a wife.

One-and-a-half years after my mother's death, my grief still spilt over at any mention of Mummy so Ranjan urged me to see a psychiatrist in Delhi. In one of the sessions, the psychiatrist asked, "Could it be that it was your mother who did you harm? Could she have wanted to bring you totally into her sphere?" I was dumbfounded. Nobody had dared put such questions to me. I went home, blocked out the questions and went to sleep.

The psychiatrist had a theory that in mourning my mother I was stuck at the age of 12. Now that Mummy was dead, the buffer shielding me from that earlier sense of desolation was gone. It was part of the history that my mother and I shared. I had never discussed it with anybody before. As I started probing, Mama Swaran said to let it be. "It's very unpleasant. Don't go deeper into it."

In the following session, the psychiatrist asked, "Does it make a difference to know that your father could have been depressed? That depression could have made a fugitive out of him? How come", he pressed, "you do not have any happy memories or affection for your father from the 12 years he spent with you?"

I began searching out details of my father's life, as I remembered him, as Ranjan and Lata saw him, as his sister knew him. I wanted to build up a case study and examine the data. I began counting the good bits, approaching it as sociological analysis, trying to examine the flip side of my story.

My father was known to be honest, sincere and truthful. My father was respected for his knowledge of medicine. He practised an old-fashioned kind of medicine. From his army days he had three standbys: Tomb's mixture for stomach aches, soda salycla for fever and colds and APC powder for fever. As a child I used to go to his clinic and help pound the tablets and fold the paper packets. One of my duties was also to dust the bottles of medicine in his cupboards.

He also had little packets of special medicine for when things got really serious. These had to be administered every 15 minutes. They were always in his black crocodile-skin medical bag. The effect was nearly instantaneous. I remember once that my roommate, Chitra, in Miranda House was ill with a high fever just before her BA exams. I called my father at his clinic. He came all the way from Khan Market to the University. She was able to do her paper the next day.

When Sunil was one-and-a-half, he caught measles and came down with a high fever in Delhi. As he suffered from febrile fits, I panicked. Pitajee came with his bag and we got Sunil through that night. It is the first time I have seen him worried, for the fever was going down very fast and Pitajee was saying, "Put the geyser on, we may need the hot water."

Pitajee was Rani's family doctor (Rani from the Refugee Block). Sitting in Ranjan's apartment in Delhi, Rani says, she would go to Pitajee and say, "Doctor Sahib, I have a cough." He would say," If you have a cough, then cough." This started all of us giving instances of my father's disdain for slight illnesses.

This casual attitude extended to his patients. I remember sitting in his clinic when a patient came in complaining of an ache. My father told her to drink some hot milk and go to sleep. He refused to give her any medicine, saying there was no need to dose oneself with medicine. It often does more harm than good. Since he had given his advice, he insisted the patient pay him the consultation fee.

His classic response to low fever was "Nobody has died of 99.2 degrees." Most of the time he was right. But one day in Khyber Pass when I felt unwell and said I felt ants going up and down my arm, my mother and father began to joke and say, "What are they making?" I went to the neighbour's house and took my temperature. It must have been over 99.2 for everybody got worried. It turned out that I had jaundice, not very severe but bad enough to put me on a fat-free diet for three months.

My cousin Jatti says:

He was too frank. One day we went to his clinic and he asked us to eat before leaving. He put the shutter down at 8 p.m. We ate. There was a knock at the door. "Who is it?" he asked.

There was an old woman and a little girl who was hurt. She had fallen down and was bleeding. "Please, Doctor Sahib, put a bandage on her head. She fell down", the woman said. Mamaji (my father) was so angry. He tied the bandage unwillingly. He said, "When the shutter is down, don't knock on the door. After I have retired, don't knock." Do you think she would come again?

Pitajee's truthfulness was often harsh and unyielding. Rani recounts that when she was around 16, her father was very sick. She went to my father and he said, "Everybody has to die one day." Rani was upset and began to cry. Rani says:

> That is the first time Doctor Sahib said sorry. Everybody said to me, "How come? Doctor Sahib never says sorry to anybody." Maybe he was trying to tell me that my father was suffering from an incurable disease, that there was no need to get so hyper and come dashing to him. But he realised then that I was too young and tender to appreciate what he was trying to say.

Rani says he always asked them to come back and tell him when they were better. He used to say, "When you are ill, you come running. When you are all right, you don't come to tell me. What is this?" This must have been instilled in Ranjan too, for in New York she went back to tell a doctor she had consulted that she was all right. The doctor scolded her for wasting his time.

In matters of religion my father was an idealist. He did not believe that there were any differences among religions. Hence that defining moment of my childhood that had us standing outside Syeda's house waiting to apologise. I also remember him taking me as a child to pay homage to the Nizamuddin Dargah (the tomb of the noted Muslim Sufi mystic), for we were one of the first families to build a house in Nizamuddin. He felt it was only proper that we ask for permission to stay. Ranjan says when the new Pir of Nizamuddin was installed, my father went to call on him, to pay his respects as one of his subjects. The new Pir was so moved that he came to my father's house to return the call.

Nevertheless, when my mother began her PhD on the Puranic influences on the Adi Granth, he found her topic to be close to heresy – tantamount to questioning the distinctive identity of Sikhism. For eight years he did not see Ranjan because she had married a Hindu. Not that she had become a Hindu, but that she had married one. When Ranjan quoted to him from the Sikh scriptures about everybody being equal in the eyes of God, he thought it was impudent that she should cite scriptures to him.

Ranjan's professor's husband, Dr Barkhuus, was at the time with the World Health Organisation in Delhi. His wife had introduced Siva and Ranjan. Dr Barkhuus went to see Pitajee and told him what a wonderful person Siva was and what a good family he came from. Ranjan says:

Pitajee kept saying, "Yes, he must be a good man." But since he was marrying his daughter, he would not see him. Dr Barkhuus looked straight at him and said, "I think, Dr Singh, you are an idiot."

Pitajee had never been called an idiot before. He later told the story to Ranjan with great pleasure.

He was a devout Sikh and wanted me to be the same. At night, he would lie down beside me before I went to sleep and tell me stories of the lives of the Sikh Gurus. I remember him saying how he had once placed four annas as an offering at the Gurdwara. That was all the money he had on him. He said he felt good for he was giving the Guru all the money he had. Yet if a beggar came to the house, he would shout loudly and do everything short of physically kicking him or her away.

He did not like questions. He also did not doubt that his truth was the only truth. Lata says that as Pitajee grew older he grew more gentle, more loving. I heard that but in my head were the sounds of Pitajee shouting. I can see him, standing in the large living room in Khyber Pass, back slightly arched, long grey beard, white turban, shouting at the servant, shouting at my mother, at me.

It came to a head one day at the dinner table. There was some sliced raw onion on a plate, together with cut tomato and whole green chillies, the traditional salad at a Punjabi meal. The servant was making *chapatis*. I was 11 and began to tell my father how my

teacher had said there was vitamin C in green chillies. This started
my father off. "No", he shouted. "Fool. There is no vitamin C in green
chillies."

I stood my ground. "Yes", I said, "Yes, there is." He turned to me,
eyes flaring, and said, "How dare you argue with me?" His voice
became shrill and hysterical. I remember sitting there knowing I had
wet my knickers.

Both my mother and I were unable in later life to bear anybody
speaking to us loudly in an imperious tone. It was as if a lever was
tripped and we were back again in Khyber Pass with my father
standing over us.

As for me, I am back where I started. Mama Swaran is right.
The story is painful and unresolved. There is no fairytale ending of
reconciliation and forgiveness. My story still remains one of hurt and
anger and complaint, mixed with some understanding as my father's
tale becomes more complex. I tell myself that my father's tragedy was
his manic depressive psychosis, that he was unsuited to his profes-
sion, that he was frustrated by his powerlessness and inability to
succeed. He was unable to deal with the challenge that his daughter's
marriage presented to the sureties of his religious and social beliefs.
His wife's growing independence and success after Partition threat-
ened his traditional role as lord and master of the house. And so he
walked out and lived the next 36 years alone, without the comforts of
a family and home. A lonely man. He lost the love of his wife and his
youngest daughter, whom he most likely loved. That was his tragedy.
He may have been surprised how for all those years I saw his story as
being about his rejection of me.

Chapter 11

The Working Girls' Hostel

––––

I don't remember my mother's first shared room in the Working Girls' Hostel. Even now when I pass by the place in Delhi which is being totally remodelled, I half turn away. It was a grim, institutional looking building, surrounded by barbed wire. It housed middle-class working women who were single because of Partition, or because they had to work to support younger siblings, or because nobody had tried to arrange their marriage. Some were like my mother – once married but single again.

A colleague at Queen Mary's School told Mummy about the Working Girls' Hostel. There was place in a shared room in D Block, the block furthest from the gate. For my mother, the hostel presented an affordable solution. My mother was paying to keep me in a hostel and subsidising my father in his clinic. She still had to complete her Master's degree, and so could only work part time. After my mother paid for the rent and food there was so little money left that if we took a three-wheeler scooter instead of the bus, it would blow the budget for the rest of the month.

The hostel was secure and offered protection. There were security men at the gate. They checked anybody coming in, including residents who entered outside the designated times. The hostel was surrounded by a high wall, embedded with barbed wire. When I stayed with my mother in her room, I felt I was being locked up inside rather than the world being kept at bay. For my mother, however, it was comforting. She was no longer the fearless woman of Partition days. She saw being without a man as being alone and without protection. "A man is a man", my mother would say, "even if he is weak or one-legged."

I used to visit her at the Working Girls' Hostel when I was in the school hostel. She must have had to ask her roommate if she minded having me there. I think both of us knew that we had to make ourselves inconspicuous in that place. As a result, I don't remember either her roommates or the shared room. The only thing I remember from that period is the canteen which used to sell milk sodas. Whenever I came from my hostel to visit her she would take me there for a treat.

A time for philosophy and poetry

It must have been 1957 when Mummy went to the Miranda House hostel to prepare for her Master's degree. She was 46. Her room was on the first floor, on the eastern side of the quadrangle. It was a liberating time, a time for study, for philosophy and poetry. There were friends with whom she discussed Punjabi and Hindi literature, the philosophy of Sikhism and Hinduism, the Bhakti movement. These discussions took place over hostel food that came from the mess in a three-tiered container eaten with rice jazzed up with cumin and ghee on an electric stove in Miss Sharma's hostel room.

My mother had become friends with Krishna Sharma. She was an historian and found in Mummy – she called her Mrs Singh – a surrogate mother and a friend. When I myself joined Miranda House a few years later and was staying in the same hostel, Miss Sharma was still there, a comforting presence in the background. Miss Sharma went on to do a doctorate on Kabir and the Bhakti movement. My mother's interest in the Bhakti movement was, of course, focused on Guru Nanak. My mother knew Kabir's work too, as it is incorporated in our holy book. I remember Mummy saying Miss Sharma had a fine mind but she kept putting things off. She finally published her thesis more than 20 years after she had completed it. I saw it in a bookshop and bought it, for I had witnessed the long gestation of this work since I was 13.

In other ways they were different. My mother was freed from the domination of her husband. Miss Sharma hankered after her own home, marriage, a husband, children. Her talk was often about her mother who had been ill for many years before she died, about her father who was old-fashioned and insisted that his daughter marry a Brahmin boy, of men who came into her life but left before she had made up her mind.

Miss Sharma had a large room with a balcony at the back, for she was a full-time lecturer. Her wardrobe was full of exquisite sarees. It was the first time I had seen so many clothes. Miss Sharma, on the other hand, was amazed when she heard that in all the years Mummy had taught at Miranda House she had owned only four sets of clothes.

Miss Sharma was the first person I heard saying that my mother was remarkable, that she had courage, that she was a scholar. Miss Sharma was my mother's first public fan and would say over and over again that I was fortunate to have a mother like her.

The visits to Miranda House when I was 13 were also my first experience of being with someone who was not from North India. My mother's neighbour in the hostel was a South Indian woman who had been married and widowed as a child. Listening to her tell Mummy of her struggles to obtain an education and financial independence first brought home to me that the stories of women in India had a common thread of sorrow. I listened to her, for I was always in the room, as that was the only place I could be. From her, I got a sense of the human dimensions of child marriage and child widows, that they were not just part of my history lessons but part of women's lives in the present day.

One day, the South Indian neighbour's uncle was visiting her. The story about him was that he had received a boon from a yogi or fakir and could read hands accurately. This gift came with the proviso that he could not profit from it or it would disappear. In his family he was much avoided for he had the habit of telling people what they did not want to know. More often than not, he was told to keep quiet if he couldn't say something positive. But my mother was taken by the idea of this uncle and wanted to know, more than anything else, whether she would get a first division in the coming MA exams.

The uncle looked at her hand and told her, no, she won't get a first division. But, he said it wouldn't make any difference because she would get good jobs. Mummy says he looked at her hand, then looked up at her and said softly, "Life has been difficult." But, he said, the last 20 years of her life would be her best years.

Back again

Mummy came back to the Working Girls' Hostel after she completed her Master's degree in 1958. She was appointed first as a part-time and then a full-time lecturer at Khalsa College at the University of Delhi. She also taught students doing their Master's in Punjabi literature at the University of Delhi. She taught at Khalsa College in Delhi for nine years. During that time, she started work on her PhD on the Puranic Influence on the Adi Granth. A Brahmin priest would come to the hostel to teach her Sanskrit.

She now had a single room. The rooms were arranged in a square with the bathrooms and toilets in a communal block at the centre. I remember the room she had in the early 1960s. There were two *nawar* beds with the traditional Punjabi red and green legs, placed in an L-shape so that they looked like two divans. She ordered a pair of red and green *khes* and used them as bedcovers. We felt pleased with ourselves for the *khes* were lovely, they were affordable and we had the gumption to place them over rather than under the sheets.

I don't remember any cupboards, so we must have had our clothes in a suitcase or trunk under the bed. But storing clothes was not a problem. Neither of us had many. Against one wall was Mummy's dressing table from Murree, the one that her Naniji had given her. It had a small swivel mirror with a drawer below it. Mummy later bought a writing desk. I still remember the man who brought it on his back from Kashmiri Gate. My mother wanted to tip him but I told her we had already paid for the delivery. Later, I saw him again as we both waited for a bus and he looked at me with the scorn I deserved.

There was a balcony at the back, where the gas stove was kept. A maid would come to wash the dishes. I think food would be delivered from outside and Mummy would modify it, as she used to do in Miranda House. We would get plenty of milk. There was curd. The left-over milk was used for rice pudding. By now we had a small fridge. We would roll out the mat and lay the food on it and sit on the floor and eat. As Mummy would have put it, these were the riches of the olden days.

We talked freely about money. I knew how much she earned, how much or how little we had in the bank. She made sure that there was always something in reserve in my bank account, so that I would never have to ask for money. I grew up feeling that there was always enough money, but also knowing that this feeling depended on not wanting more than I could have. I grew up with a sense of "our money", with the financial unit being defined just by my mother and me. For me, it was bounded richness, not the kind of spilling over abundance that she had known in Nanaji's house. My mother always retained some sense of that spilling over quality.

We talked of her study and mine, of religion and philosophy and poetry, sociology and anthropology. I thought a mother was always an intellectual companion. My image of her was always of those years when I was at university and she lived in the Working Girls' Hostel, teaching and studying. It set my template for a good life, which had to be of the mind. We lost that kind of communion, first when I went to Malaysia and sank into a dull listlessness without work and intimacy. We got it back again for a while when she was in Patti and I had begun writing and studying. But then in the last ten years of her life, she receded from intellectual life and I could not share her comfort in religious practice.

By the mid-1960s, friends would also come to stay. I had got over my embarrassment that I did not have a "real" home. All the years I was at school, I didn't ever volunteer the information that my mother stayed in the Working Girls' Hostel. I joined Miranda House as a boarder in 1960 to do my BA Honours in English Literature – tracing my mother's footsteps – and didn't talk of it even then. However, my group of friends knew because my mother was always a very welcome visitor. One year my roommate needed a place to stay because she could not go home for the vacation, and she announced that she was coming to stay with us at the hostel. So, without discussion, because my friends treated the hostel as my home, I began to do the same.

Kin networks

Mama Khojinder, Mamiji and my cousins would come and visit us at the hostel. Mamiji remembers that Mummy used to be so pleased to see them. She would take them to her canteen. In this females-only enclave, Mamaji must have been left to sit in the visitors' room. It was "very tasty tea, *samosas* and *gulab jamun*", Mamiji says. "It was wonderful. We loved having it." Mama Swaran was in Delhi and we would go to stay with him sometimes. But Mummy tried not to behave like a needy sister-in-law wanting succour.

Bapuji's family was a constant in my mother's life. We visited Bapuji's son, Harbans, in Delhi and stayed often. When Professor Thakur Singh came, he stayed there, and so did we.

We often saw Masi Darshan and her children. They too must have moved innumerable times. My mother and Masi Darshan had much in common. My father and Masi Darshan's husband were first cousins. Both women were now alone. Masi Darshan, six years younger, was in a sense worse off for she had to bring up three young children. But she had the support of the man she had wanted to marry. He never married and remained an anchor for her and her children.

Happy times – visiting Mama Khojinder in Pune in 1956

For my mother, kinship was still the framework for social relationships. She related to three sets of *paikai* – her brothers, her mother's kin and Bapuji's family. Her maternal cousins continued to be important. They were well established in Delhi and were the ones who helped us financially and with goods. We were always on the receiving side. But I did not sense any social distance between Mummy and them. For these cousins, my mother was always the older sister they had played with in their grandfather's house in Rawalpindi. Particularly with Masi Deep, there was much mutual love and caring. We often visited their large house on Bhagwan Das Road, where they kept a gracious Westernised establishment complete with bearers in livery. I remember a green-and-white-striped swinging couch with cushions, a Great Dane sitting beside it, and liveried bearers serving us tea in the garden. Invariably their chauffeur would drop us back. But none of them would visit us at the Working Girls' Hostel.

My kinship network was narrow. Some of it was because of Partition. Unlike my mother and sisters, I had no experience of kin living together in the same locality. Differences in economic status and age became unbridgeable without this constant meeting at family functions. Some of it was because our home had dissolved and I spent the next nine years in school and university hostels.

My maternal kin were my mother's brothers and their families and Masi Darshan and her family. I remember my mother's maternal cousins fondly and often went with her to visit them, but I did not have any relationship with their children. When I did see them, it was in their homes but we came from different worlds. I left India before we could establish relationships as adults.

My sisters are close to their paternal kin. For me, my father's kin became secondary when he left home. I met his kin at his clinic or if I went with him to visit them. None of them came to visit me. Moreover, all the children of my paternal aunts and of my father's cousins were years older than I was.

So, for me, friendship rather than kinship became the sustaining metaphor of human connection. Friends became family and I related with the families of my friends. My friends would often visit my mother even when I was not there. For my mother too, friends were important. In her 19 years in Dharamshala, her friends became like family – she was the mother with daughters and sons scattered around the Sikh community. Her networks, whether kin or friends, remained connected. One day when I began to chart my networks of family and friends, I realised that only my family networks were connected. The others were single points of relationship.

Living with my mother again

I completed my BA (Hons) from Miranda House in 1963 and then my Masters in Sociology from the Delhi School of Economics in 1965. I spent five years at the Miranda House hostel, visiting my mother often at the Working Girls' Hostel. My mother continued to teach at Khalsa College and at the University of Delhi. I then went for a year on scholarship to Drew University in Madison, New Jersey, to do my Masters in Political Science, spending a term in London and two months hitch-hiking in Europe. My mother moved on to become the Acting Principal of Mata Sundari College in Delhi.

I came back from the United States in early 1967 and moved in with Mummy in the Working Girls' Hostel and began working at the Institute of Economic Growth at the University of Delhi. Life was pleasant. There was sufficient money. There was good conversation at work and at home. Work was fun. I had a large room to myself at work where I did research and was able to borrow as many books as I wanted from the library. At 4 p.m. every evening all of us would have tea in the staff room, where I would listen to older colleagues telling inside stories of government and cabinet decision making.

The Delhi School of Economics was next door, which meant comfort and old friends were close by. Some of my friends from Miranda House were now working in other colleges on the University campus. We had money of our own to spend for the first time. Friends would stop by to pick me up at the Working Girls' Hostel for coffee at the 24-hour coffee shop at the Oberoi Hotel. It was then the "in" place to be.

We would go off on trips out of Delhi. Bonny, my room mate in Miranda House, and I went to Hardwar and stayed in an *ashram* overnight by the Ganges in Rishikesh. At dusk, we floated oil lamps on the river. Another time we went to see the Khajurao temples, presenting ourselves at Bonny's aunt's place in Hansi for board and lodging.

We spent part of the summer in Kotgarh at Sunita's family's apple orchards. Sunita had been in the Miranda House hostel with me. Mummy came with us too, for she knew Sunita well as Sunita had stayed with us at the Working Girls' Hostel. My mother re-lived her childhood experience of picking fruit from their cherry trees. Mummy went back to Delhi while the rest of us went on to Mandi, Kulu, Manali, Rohtang Pass, Kashmir. We stayed at friends' houses, or friends' friends' houses, cheap hotels and Gurdwaras.

Another trip I took by myself was to Bihar to dig wells with Service Civil International, living in a village for the first time. On the way, I dropped off at Patna and went to Patna Sahib, the birthplace of our tenth guru, Guru Gobind Singh Ji. I crossed the Ganges and was part of a wedding party with an elephant and dancing girls. I ended up hitching a ride on a truck with an Indian man I had met on the train and went to Khatmandu. On the way back, I went to the village and then went on to ostensibly visit my uncle near Calcutta, but spent most of my time with an economist I had met earlier at a seminar in Simla. India seemed wide open and I was exploring my own country.

A dismal place

The Working Girls' Hostel continued to be a dismal place. It had the odour of failed dreams. It housed people whose lives had not worked out. Most of the women did not earn enough to have a wholly independent life style, even if it were socially possible. Many had lovers who were married and who would come faithfully every evening to sit in the visitors' room, where the women would offer them sweetmeats they had made for them. Then the married lovers would go back to their families. In some cases this was an agreed and open arrangement between the man, his wife and his mistress. In others, it was the cause of much heartache.

There were women who lived together, sharing a room. Only

later, I wondered whether many of these were lesbian relationships. At the time, the only thing people would say was, "There is much love between these two women. Isn't it lovely how they care for each other?"

We had tried to rent a house once I began working at the University. But things had not changed much between 1956 and 1967. Landlords would still not rent a flat to two women. I remember we went to a middle-class area near the University. When the landlord heard there was no man with us, he said, "If I rent the house to you, all the *lafenge* [bawdy men] in town will circle the place." It was as if we were bitches on heat. I was then 23 and my mother was 56. We did not try again.

My way out of the Working Girls' Hostel was to get married. I was afraid I would become one of those wasted women pining for a home and family. In December 1967 I agreed to an arranged marriage. I was 23½.

An arranged marriage

My mother had tried to arrange my marriage when I was doing my Masters in Delhi, and again after I returned from the United States. She hoped for it, but it was not something she expected would happen. I had too many strikes against me. Separated parents. No home. Father a manic-depressive. If anybody had probed, there were several manic-depressives on my mother's side as well. Not too much money. Yes, I was fair and tall. This meant that by Punjabi standards I was beautiful. But was I too educated with two Masters degrees? Too Western? Too feminist? Too opinionated?

There was no question of my mother trying to press an arranged marriage on me. The routine was that there would be a tea at an uncle's house. I would be told that a "boy" was coming to see me. I expected a mismatch. The men in my mother's social circle were often in the army and sought girls who would make good traditional wives. For them, I was too educated. For me, they were often not educated enough.

In 1967 a match was proposed through an unusual route. My

mother's Professor of Punjabi Literature had visited Malaysia and stayed with a family in Penang. When the grandmother from that family came looking for a match for her eldest grandson, Mummy's professor thought of me. He knew the boy's family was decent, well off and highly regarded in the community. The man, we heard, was a gynaecologist, had studied in Delhi and Edinburgh.

I was ready to consider an arranged marriage, for I hadn't been good at arranging my own. Some years before, I had fallen in love with a fellow student from Trinidad. In my mind, love meant marriage. I assumed I was engaged, though I can't remember him asking directly. Prem Singh looked after him for a while in the flat he had rented. My sister came down from Bombay to look him over. I took him to see my father. My father liked him, but of course stopped speaking to me for the man was Christian. The guy left for home and wrote to me from Aden breaking off the relationship.

I went to the US, came back and was briefly infatuated with a Bengali economist who was a Naxalite. It was romantic but I knew I was his bourgeois fling and he was my attempt at living dangerously. So when this Malaysian arranged match was suggested, all of us in the family discussed it and wondered that perhaps it was worth a try. It was a calculated risk. I had an education and could always look after myself if it didn't work. We approached it as a risk management strategy, giving me the veto. None of us asked what kind of life I wanted and what kind of person I wanted to live with. I didn't either. I knew I did not want the Working Girls' Hostel.

Charan, the "boy" who was being proposed, seemed to have a background that was a combination of the Indian and the Western. He matched me educationally. The family was known to my mother's professor. Moreover, the boy's grandmother was related to Mami Mohinder's sister's in-laws. The family was of the Pindi Ahluwalia baradari. This was more a question of connection rather than an essential requirement for us. But it was interesting how the old marriage boundaries stuck. The match was worth investigation. Photographs were exchanged. We sent him my photograph, one that Ranjan had taken of me in New York. She was trying to show off the curtains she had sewn and I was standing to the side, looking demure.

The next step was to meet. The meeting was more a veto occasion than a romantic situation – if we did not like each other, the matter would stop. As a default, my friend Priya from Miranda House days and I had a trip planned to Uttarkashi, the mouth of the Ganges.

Once it was a possibility, Charan came down from Penang, prepared to marry, with a diamond ring and some nylon sarees embroidered with gold. Nandy, Lata's husband went to see him. When Charan had passed that hurdle, my mother and I went "for tea" to her professor's house. We talked for a while and I heard that he liked folk tales. I thought he couldn't be all bad if he liked folk tales.

We met the next day at the University. A journalist friend was visiting me at the time. Charan was taken aback at my ease with him. I didn't pay too much attention to his reaction. We went to the Hotel Oberoi for coffee, and Charan didn't care for my choice of a hamburger. He asked whether it was a beef hamburger and I told him I had not asked. There was silence, and I remember paying a lot more attention to a bird in a cage than to him. Despite these fumbles, in the taxi as we returned to the University, he proposed and I accepted. We got married within seven days.

Of course we didn't tell him that my father was manic-depressive. Or that I was headstrong and impatient with authority, or that I would not take kindly to patriarchal dominance. I did not tell him I defined myself by my excellence in education, or that I had been in love at least once before. I did not even know myself that I was terrified of being abandoned. Charan assumed that with a marriage arranged in India, he would get a traditional girl who would be soft-spoken and submissive. The education was just supposed to be a little extra gloss for marketing purposes, nothing that could have shaped the mind. Later, he said, only half in joke, we had fooled him with that demure photograph. Long after our divorce, he told me he had screened more than 90 Delhi girls with a view to marriage. He rejected some of them because they had hair on their arms, others because they were not tall or fair enough. And after all that, he said, appreciating the joke was on him, "I got you."

Charan didn't tell us that he wasn't 32 as his grandmother had said, but 37. He also didn't tell us that he was a general practitioner and had not passed the exams to become a Member of the Royal College of Obstetricians and Gynaecologists, which would have made him a specialist. He had told nobody that he liked playing poker and mahjong and lost at both.

My mother was able to organise my wedding, the only traditional wedding in the family. She had wedding cards printed but I found them later in her cupboard as she hadn't had time to distribute them. Bapuji came from Tarn Taran to do the *ardas* for the marriage, even though Charan had a trimmed beard. He said that if the *jatha* fined him for attending, he would accept the fine. Ranjan and Siva hastily came from New York. We waited for them to start the wedding. I came out with my two sisters, dressed in a traditional pink and gold saree, with my great-grandmother's *bagh* draped over it. I wore my mother's ruby necklace, which was now mine.

The wedding went well. The honeymoon was good too. I left Delhi for Penang, with a suitcase full of ritual gifts for my in-laws, sarees for me, wearing the red and white bangles of a new bride. My books were sent by sea in the trunk Ranjan had given me in New York. It is now an antique in my son Sunil's house.

Within a fortnight I knew I had chosen unwisely. I should have gone to Uttarkashi instead.

"You will make yourself bankrupt"

Whenever anybody asked my mother whether they should marry their daughters overseas, she told them not to do it. "You will make yourself bankrupt", she would say. "Send your daughter away and you lose her."

We didn't quite lose each other but the everyday rhythm of life is hard to communicate, especially if you don't want to tell the whole story or even recognise it yourself. I learned that early on, for a letter which spoke of unhappiness worried her for weeks after I had forgotten the incident. Telephone calls from Penang to Delhi were not the norm in the late 1960s. Writing was also a problem. I did not read Gurmukhi fluently and English continued to remain difficult for my mother. I remember the air letter forms that would come, written large and bold in English, lovely to receive, but only containing the spot news.

I became involved in coping with a new country, my husband and children, and lost touch with her life. Penang was exotic, with orchids and bougainvillea and frangipani. Charan's family was welcoming. His mother had died the year before our marriage. Everybody had wonderful things to say of her. Without her, the family had lost its social and relationship centre. Charan's father had come to Malaysia as a draughtsman, worked with his sister's husband and made his money through money lending and investment.

My family, of course, did not know about the money lending connection in the family. We did not even ask, for Sikhs in India are not associated with money lending. In my mind, that world was part of Premchand's novels, where the Bania is the evil money lender. I did not know at the time about the Sikh money lenders in Rawalpindi. In Malaysia, money lending was the Sikh road to prosperity. They say that if you check the land records you will nearly always find a Bengali (the Malaysian term for North Indian) or Chettiar name on the title.

My in-laws lived in a large double-storey house with a flowering garden with orchids, frangipani and mussaenda in front and rambutan trees at the back. Bibiji, my grandmother-in-law, had planted a neem tree (Azadirachta indica) and had a tulsi (holy basil) plant in a pot. Two Tamil girls of 16 looked after the house. Charan's younger sister and brother lived on the ground floor. Charan and I had a unit on the first floor with its own bathroom. Across the corridor was Trip, the brother closest to Charan in age. He had been married and divorced and had two children. His wife had left for Delhi with the children. So my father-in-law was apprehensive as to whether this marriage would last.

Neither my family nor I had anticipated the differences between Sikhs in Delhi and Sikhs in Malaysia. Most of the Malaysian Sikhs came from villages and small towns in Punjab more than half a century ago and rose from positions in the police or as security guards. The second generation had been educated and became professionals. As a result, Sikhs in Malaysia spoke an antiquated and rustic Punjabi specific to their native villages at the time when they left India.

It is difficult to play the anthropologist with your own life. The first time I heard one of the women who had gathered around me as a new bride talk of my clothes as *leerai* ("rags" in my Delhi version of Punjabi), I retreated to my room upstairs. I heard these cadences – a mixture of strange Punjabi and Malay – and was unable to face the strange when I had expected the familiar. For me, the differences were crystallised when I heard Charan's brother-in-law address his mother with the familiar *tu* rather than the respectful *tusi*. My reaction was so sharp that it began my retreat from speaking Punjabi in Malaysia. The same differences in language delighted my mother. When she visited us in Penang in 1969, she marvelled at this living museum of old Punjabi.

To the family and the Sikhs I met in Penang, India was *des*, the country, the home country. It was the reference point for their customs. So getting a bride from *des* was getting the genuine product, like *desi ghee*. Other than Indian films and music, *des* meant Punjab. I did not know Punjab. In Delhi, I identified myself as an Indian, having friends from all over India, going to music and dance recitals, and reading the regional literature in India, wherever it was available. Before my marriage I was learning Kathak in the evenings and was planning to study Tamil in the mornings.

There was no university in Penang at the time. I had never been in a place where there was no university. I don't think I had asked. We also hadn't been aware that my degrees from India and the United States would not be recognised in the Malaysia of the 1960s. Apart from American Ivy League universities and a few medical colleges in India, Malaysia recognised only British universities.

No milk was delivered to the house. A Punjabi would not think of asking, "Will there be milk?" I used to drink only milk at home before

I was married. But in Malaysia at the time, Malays and Chinese did not generally drink milk. Some are indeed lactose-intolerant. It was not until the 1980s that flavoured milk appeared in supermarkets. There were some Punjabi milkmen but we must have lived outside their circuit. So we used evaporated milk in tea and coffee.

Though I found it difficult to connect with the Punjabi culture in Malaysia, I reached out to experience the Malay and Chinese worlds. Charan did not have Malay friends who visited the house, but Daddy, Charan's father, had lived in Perlis in north Malaysia. Over the dinner table, he told stories of *bomohs* (medicine men) and black magic, which is prevalent along the Malaysian-Thai border. Charan had a close Chinese friend and we attended his wedding tea ceremony, because I asked.

The Chinese part of town was new for me. As a family, particularly when I was a new bride, we would go to Chinese restaurants in town and by the sea and Daddy would order the festive suckling pig. The first time I was given the kidneys, which were the delicacy. The men would have the best brandy with 7-Up in it, the usual way of drinking brandy in Malaysia at the time. The women would order fresh orange juice and after a while switch to Chinese tea. Sitting at a round table trying to eat with chopsticks seemed an adventure.

Every visit to the vegetable market was a discovery. At times there would be Chinese opera sponsored by the stallholders. At other times I had warm soya bean curd with brown sugar. A Tamil woman who sat at the front of the vegetable market would help me make the best crabs by giving me the exact amount of curry paste I needed for the amount I had bought. Crabs were new to me and I had to learn how to clean them. In fact, cooking at all was new to me. I bought Mrs Balbir Singh's cook book and followed it so slavishly that Daddy asked whether it was written that I first had to turn on the stove.

In June 1969, my mother came to Penang. My father-in-law had organised a lecture tour for her in Malaysia and Singapore on the occasion of Guru Nanak Dev Ji's 500th birth anniversary. I had not realised that it was unusual for a woman scholar to address the Sikh congregation in Malaysia. Thirty-two years later, in 2001, when I went back to the Penang Gurdwara for Sunil's wedding, two women asked about my mother.

I took my mother on one of the trishaws to show her Penang, the usual way I travelled to the city. Mummy enthused about the temples, the shops, the exotic flavour of the town, and then asked, "Is this as fast as it gets?" Charan and his family were gracious hosts. I was pregnant with my first child. I don't know how much of the rest of my life she glimpsed.

My mother went back to Delhi and soon after moved to Amritsar to become the founding principal of Khalsa College for Women. In March 1970, she had a heart attack, and I went to Amritsar with Aman, my four-month-old son. Ranjan had also come from New York. She noticed I was not wearing my diamond ring and so the family discovered that my jewellery had been pawned to pay money lenders for my husband's gambling debts. While in Amritsar, I discovered I was pregnant with Sunil.

I had family support to choose whatever path I wanted. I chose to go back to Penang until I was able to provide a home and financial choices for myself and my children. In the meantime, my mother made sure I had a pound of liver every day I was with her so I would be less weak and anaemic when I left.

Chapter 12

Principal Inder Kaur

———

When my mother was invited to become the Founding Principal of Khalsa College for Women in Amritsar in 1969, she was doing well in Delhi but was glad to leave. It was unlikely she would become the Principal of Mata Sundari College where she had been teaching. After 12 years living in the Working Girls' Hostel she found herself pleading with God, "Enough. It is enough. Twelve years is enough." Soon after, the Khalsa College committee approached her. They were establishing a sister college to the historic Khalsa College that has been part of Sikh history. My mother must have been an ideal candidate with postgraduate qualifications, an experiential knowledge of the scriptures, and administrative and leadership experience. Moreover, at 58, she gave the new institution a look of immediate respectability and maturity.

Working in Delhi, 1969

The only problem was that they were offering less pay than she was receiving in Delhi. But Pitajee said Mummy should take it in acknowledgment of the honour being bestowed on her. She would also have to defer completing her PhD. That wasn't going well, for her supervisor had moved to Punjab, and she was beginning to think that if she wanted to continue, she would have to change her dissertation topic. But she later realised that at that time she had chosen a career as an educator over achieving her personal goal of doing her PhD.

Leaving Delhi

My mother left Delhi in 1969, where she had lived for 21 years, to return to Punjab. She also returned to Bapuji's family. Professor Thakur Singh was now in charge of physical education at Khalsa College and his house was in the college compound, across a fence from my mother's house. Bapuji was just an hour away in Tarn Taran.

Becoming the principal of a college was the fulfilment of a dream she had almost dared not dream. She liked her letters addressed to her as Principal Inder Kaur. I saw it as a natural progression. My mother had studied and taught all my life. So it was right that she was the principal of a college now. She went on to start two other women's colleges in Punjab, in Lopon and Patti.

I remember little of her time as Principal of Khalsa College, except that she lived in the principal's bungalow. She had vegetables growing in the garden. She had a gardener. She was finally able to welcome Ranjan and Siva to her home. She insisted that a urinal be built in the bathroom, thinking it was an essential part of the Western toilet. I don't think Siva even mentioned that the urinal was installed too high.

I saw her as the Principal, at the pinnacle of her career. I wasn't aware that she had to counter the moves of younger women who wanted to take over the position as my mother approached 60. I did not know the subtleties of working in Punjab, where even professional relationships are couched in the idiom of family. When the Management Committee did not want to give my mother the three-year-extension she requested, she decided to leave. She told the Committee, "My husband does not agree to my working any longer. My children do not agree. My doctors do not agree."

Lopon

Soon after, my mother was invited to become the founding principal of the first women's college in Lopon. It was the first time girls from the villages around were able to get a university education. To me, Lopon seemed to be in the middle of nowhere. Moga was the closest town. At first, Mummy had baulked at this isolation. But there was a large Gurdwara in Lopon, and it was the Gurdwara that had sought her out. Professor Thakur Singh came to settle her in and meet with the religious head of the Gurdwara.

Aman, Sunil and I came from Sandakan in Borneo to visit her in Lopon in 1972. My memories of Lopon are of the pomegranate grove near the women's college and a buffalo calf that Aman and Sunil called Brownie. But the boys cried all the time. I was not used to running after them. They were nearly two and three. At home, a lovely Malay girl, Intah, used to run after them. As a result, they spoke a mixture of Malay, Punjabi and English that nobody in Lopon understood. We were all miserable, but the young teachers kept telling us what wonderful children they were. Mummy hired a young girl from a nearby village to play with the boys. She and her sisters stayed and looked after my mother for the next 20 years.

We had to leave Lopon hastily on a *tempo* with people hanging on to the sides, to go to Ludhiana and then Delhi, for both boys caught the measles and had the high fever that accompanies the disease.

Patti

When Mummy was 65, she had to retire from Lopon according to university regulations. By this time the college had a university-approved BEd program. She thought she would now go to Chandigarh and complete her PhD under her old supervisor. But then the Gurdwara in Patti approached her – through Bapuji's grandson, Bakshi – to establish a college for women. Patti was an hour-and-a-half by train from Amritsar and nearly as close to Tarn Taran.

Again, it was the first college to serve the town and the 52 villages around it. She remained there for 10 years and finally retired when she was 75. Unlike Amritsar and Lopon, the college in Patti is floundering due to a lack of financial support. The sun-drenched courtyard is still there, the *pakoras* from the nearby shops are still as hot. Some of the teachers my mother hired remain. This is more out of a sense of service than anything else, for they have not been paid for a year.

Principal Inder Kaur in Patti

When Aman, Sunil and I visited her in Patti in 1977, Mummy's main worry was the toilets. How would her grandsons cope with the commodes on the roof? But Aman and Sunil thought the commodes were great. They had never seen a roof which was also the social centre of the house. It was a tall, narrow house with steep stairs. My mother occupied the second floor, and there was yet another floor between her and the roof. I remember rice pudding being made every day, especially for Aman, who developed a passion for it. The children were now six and seven and would also spend hours at the bedroom window looking down at the cobbled streets, watching camels and horses go by.

We took a *tonga*, a horse-driven cart, to visit a farm nearby that belonged to Bapuji's granddaughter. The children sat in the front and Mummy and I were at the back that sloped downwards. The roads were rough and unpaved, but the man seemed to want to prove that his mare was made for galloping. Every time Mummy told him to slow down, he remonstrated and made the mare go faster.

The children were delighted but my mother and I held on tight and finally arrived to a farm full of pear trees and parrots. Nobody was at home.

Mummy wears a dastar

While in Patti, Mummy began to wear the *dastar*, a navy blue small turban worn by the women of Bapuji's *jatha*. You have to take your hair up and make a small bun at the top of the head. The turban goes around that covering the hair. To the rest of her family in Delhi, this seemed to be the final betrayal. Now Mummy didn't even look like one of us. She now belonged to Bapuji's family rather than ours.

Bapuji had not asked Mummy to wear the *dastar*. But in Patti, many men from the *jatha* would come every week to do *kirtan* in the Patti Gurdwara. In Patti everyone regarded Mummy as Bapuji's daughter. Mummy would be invited to do the *kirtan*. She said, "The Singhs did not say anything but I myself felt ashamed that being his daughter I did not wear a *dastar*."

Mummy went to see Bapuji's granddaughter, Banta, and her husband, Dhillon Sahib, and told them she wanted to wear a *dastar* at the *akhand paath* she was holding to honour her aunt Jasram (Masi Darshan's mother who had helped bring up Mummy), who had died in the mental home in Ranchi. When they came for the *akhand paath*, they brought a *dastar* with them. Bapuji had also come. He said to Mummy, "Bibi, it is my great happiness that you wore the *dastar* because of me."

Then Lata arrived in Patti for a visit. Of course Mummy had not written to her about the *dastar*. Mummy said:

Lata saw me and said, "What have you done? What is this?" I said "This is a *dastar*." She was very upset. She said, "Now this is a new thing you have done. You have to go to University, meet educated people. Now what will they think? How can you do this?" I said, "Yes, yes. It is right." She kept getting more and more angry.

Mummy laughs, recounting it. "I put the cooler on also", she said.

But Lata continued, "You mustn't wear this and come to Delhi."

Lata stayed two nights. The next day she told Mummy she could stay another night. Mummy said, "No you have made your program, you have said you will go, you should go." She did not want to deal with Lata's anger for another day. "Lata thought she had said her piece and that it would influence me. But it didn't. I said, 'Yes, Yes.' So what happened? She went back to her house, I was in mine. What could happen?"

In Delhi the family thought Mummy had lost it, that she was on the slippery slope to fanaticism. It was about this time she stopped eating eggs. She also gave up tea, to which she had been addicted. Surprisingly the *jatha* thought coffee was all right.

When I came to Delhi for a visit, I went berserk seeing my mother in fundamentalist garb. I had cut my hair around 1974 when I was in Sandakan. My hair was no longer as thick as it had been. I thought I would also look more attractive with cut hair. I knew that by cutting my hair I was infringing Sikh traditional values, that I would no longer be regarded as an initiated Sikh. I had never understood why hair was accorded such an important place in Sikh religion but it was not something my mother or father would discuss.

I did not confront my father with my cut hair. When I went to see him I would put on a hair piece. Lata said it was fine for me to do what I wanted but she didn't want to have to pick up the pieces after I left. So I kept faking it. I think he knew but we did not discuss it.

Of course Mummy was shocked when I told her. But it was a choice – have me on my terms or I would stay in Delhi and not visit her in Patti. She quickly decided she could handle it. So she reminded me that it was a bit precious for me to throw a fit upon seeing her in a *dastar*. Mummy says I gave her a long lecture, saying I had thought she was a modern, broad-minded Sikh, and now, look at her, just part of a sect!

Mummy put up with me haranguing her for two or three days. In the mornings she would attend *kirtan* by the *jatha*. In the evenings she would come back and listen to me and the rest of us. After the first two days, she said, "All right. You have cut your hair. Did you ask me? If you did not ask me, I don't have to ask you either. It was my wish. I did it."

She topped that with a histrionic, "If you are so upset, think you don't have a mother. I am going to remain like this. You like your mother, it is all right. You don't like it, I will go."

That silenced me. We began to talk. She said she now felt more comfortable with herself, felt that she belonged to the family and group around her. Mummy felt there was a rightness about her looking like the rest of the family, Bapuji's family. Everybody in Patti and outside was now more respectful.

Of course then I asked, "Why didn't you say this before? Why didn't you stand your ground from the beginning instead of playing these traditional games?" We rolled around laughing, as she told me how difficult it was in the beginning to comb her hair upwards. Her head would hurt. Later of course, she found her head would hurt when she combed her hair down.

Bapuji dies

Bapuji died in Amritsar on 23 July 1979. Mummy had been with him for two days and two nights. The evening before his death, Bapuji had difficulty breathing. The doctor gave him an injection and told the family there was little to worry about. The breathing difficulty was because some of the orange juice had gone the wrong way. The family was relieved. They persuaded Mummy to go to Patti for a day to attend to college matters.

Mummy returned to Patti. The night passed without her being able to sleep. The 7 o'clock train to Amritsar left. The 11 o'clock train left. Mummy abided by the program she had made and did her duties in the college. She waited for the 3 p.m. train. It was late. But then a telephone call came to the house upstairs. They had taken Bapuji's body to Tarn Taran and the cremation was at 5 p.m.

In Tarn Taran hundreds of devotees had gathered in front of the house. Hymns were being sung. Mummy asked, "Is this it?" The bier was carried past Tarn Taran Sahib, the venerated Gurdwara. Flowers from the temple were placed on the body. The whole town followed behind. After the cremation, the prayers began at home. Night fell. Prayers continued the next day and night. In her grief, she became stubborn, upbraiding Bapuji, "Why didn't you meet me before going? You always told me I was your most loved child. Was this your love? You sent me away from hospital and then flew away without meeting me."

Then she took another tack. "It is true there is the ultimate will. But you are a great soul. You could have said you wanted to see me first. Why did you go away without meeting me? Why did you go?" Like a child she wept, her tears soaking the pillow. She was beside herself and kept accusing Bapuji, holding him to account. "That was your love? Was that it?"

She drifted off for a few moments in her grief. Then she felt her forehead being stroked from the right to the left, her being suffused with loving care. She then heard Bapuji's voice addressing her with the Sikh greeting, "*Wahe Guruji ka Khalsa, Wahe Guruji ki Fateh.* The Khalsa belongs to the Lord. The victory belongs to the Lord." He said, "Now meet me." This was her Bapuji's voice. Her tears of grief turned to tears of thanksgiving.

I listen to my mother writing of Bapuji's death in the book on his life to which she contributed, and wonder how it was possible that I did not know this was one of the most traumatic moments in my mother's life. I also don't remember particularly taking note of Professor Thakur Singh's death ten years later. Was I particularly insensitive and self-centred? She must have written about these events to me or my sister must have written.

I hope I wrote to her. But 1979 was a period in limbo, just before my move from Borneo to Kuala Lumpur and then filing for divorce.

Mummy continued at Patti for another seven years. But her eyesight had begun to fail soon after Bapuji's death. She could not recognise the boundaries of things, so could not read ordinary-sized print. In 1986, she left Patti to settle in Amritsar in a set of rooms opposite Banta's house (Bapuji's grand-daughter). It was close enough for Banta to bring my mother something hot from her kitchen, and for my mother to amble over to discuss theology with

Banta's husband Dhillon Sahib in the morning sun. Bapuji's son, Kulwant, lived down the road and Tarn Taran was only an hour away. Professor Thakur Singh had retired by this time and was living with his youngest daughter, Pashi, in Amritsar. And of course, the main attraction was the Golden Temple, Harmandir Sahib. This is where my mother wanted to end her days.

Chapter 13

A disconnect

_____

While my mother was in Lopon and Patti, I was in Sandakan, East Malaysia. We had moved there shortly after Sunil's birth in 1971. The move offered better professional prospects for Charan and an allowance for working in East Malaysia. I also thought it might give us a new chance at a relationship away from the poker tables.

The wrong side of Borneo

I was excited about going to Borneo, having studied the Ibans in Social Anthropology in Delhi. Only later, I realised I had landed on the wrong side of Borneo, for the Ibans were in Sarawak on the western side of the island and we were in Sabah in the north-east. Sandakan was predominantly a Hakka town. In the villages fringing the sea were Sulus and Simunuls. The main indigenous groups of Sabah, the Kadazans and Muruts, were further west and inland.

I found Sandakan different from anywhere else I had been. It was a small town compared with Penang. It was remote, and living in Borneo had a sense of romance associated with it. There were only four Punjabi families in Sandakan. In Sandakan I tried for the first time to become Malaysian and sought to belong to my adopted country. I went back to school and passed Bahasa Malaysia at the school certificate level. Soon after we arrived, I asked around for a Mandarin teacher. A few days later, Ie Lien arrived. She wanted to improve her spoken English, and would teach me Mandarin in return. This started my journey in a tonal language, which in the beginning I was unable to hear. In the end, Ie Lien had to conduct me – the word goes up, down, flat, up and down. Getting the tone right was essential because the meaning becomes different depending on tones and it is also written differently. I began to learn to read and write Mandarin, but without any immediate use for writing and due to its complexity, I settled for being able to speak it. Because Ie Lien was a graduate of Chinese literature and spoke with the Beijing accent, people commended me for my educated accent.

There was a grand old Punjabi woman who became a friend. Through her, I learnt about Sandakan in the early days of the 20th century, how she had come there as a bride to a much older man who herded buffaloes, how they had learnt to make *chapatis* from *maida* (refined flour) during the Japanese occupation and continued to do so. I also slowly got to know the Simunul village of Kampung Bokara, fifteen minutes away from the town. Here I met Emmong, the matriarch of a large kin group. Later, I lived in the village for eight months learning their language and customs. This was part of my attempt to do an MA which would be recognised in Malaysia and so get back to university and earn a living, though there was no university at the time in the whole of Sabah.

Sabah became part of Malaysia in 1963 but it still had a colonial flavour. There was a Resident in Sandakan. The senior officers of Harrison & Crossfield and the Standard Chartered Bank were from the United Kingdom, in a throwback to Somerset Maugham days. Together they formed the nucleus of the establishment. To this layer were added the top echelons of the civil service and the professions. As Charan soon became head of the Sandakan Hospital, we became part of the group who stood around at parties. I cooked "curry" for their visiting relatives from the United Kingdom. This bit of Sandakan did not work for me. I did not make a single friend in that crowd.

I began to write occasionally for the *The New Straits Times*, at that time the premier Malaysian English newspaper. I tried to communicate the flavour of my life as a housewife with two children in Sandakan. In this way, I also described my life in Borneo to my mother.

Becoming Malaysian

The children and I travelled. We went along the mangrove swamps of Sandakan Bay, in the guano caves where the nests of swiftlets are harvested, along the large Kinabatangan river. I was enjoying my children. They were old enough to take with me wherever I wanted to go. They gave me the freedom to roam, which would not otherwise have been possible for a woman alone in Borneo. We visited friends of friends on the west coast to celebrate the Kadazan festivals, went to Bajau markets, travelled inland to visit Muruts in their long-houses, walked over swinging bridges over fast-flowing rivers, and saw turtles coming in to lay their eggs on the same beach year after year. We went on fishing trawlers and ate fish we had caught.

It was a good time. I was in a new country and I was making it mine. I was young. My children were growing up carefree in a town which then had only 40,000 people. They had the freedom of a large playing field in front of the house, the swimming pool in the club nearby, a library across the road and the hills and jungle at the back. The marriage was still bad but it counted for less. The poker had been replaced by mahjong in the club across the road. It was still desolate to be abandoned night after night but now that I was writing I was not so alone with myself. The writing also gave me some money of my own for the first time during my marriage. That was important, for I never found it easy to ask for money.

As soon as Sunil was old enough to go to primary school, the children and I left for Kuala Lumpur. Ostensibly it was to register for further study at the University of Malaya. But I had got out. I went to the editor of *The New Straits Times* and found that in all the years I had been writing alone in Sandakan, I had become a star. I was that rare phenomenon much loved by editors – an ordinary housewife who wrote about everyday things. Soon I had enough freelance work at the paper to keep me fully occupied.

I was now in a world totally different from my mother's, with few points in common. We saw her seldom. The visits to Lopon and Patti had been the only ones we had made in the 1970s. The children were growing up without getting to know their grandmother and without many memories of India. What would remain of such memories as they had and from later visits was a feeling that India was a special, though foreign, place.

At the end of 1978, we went back to Sandakan. I went to Kampung Bokara to do my field work. It was a way of furthering my studies and also being away from my marriage. Charan did not want the children to be with me in the village, so they remained with him and went to the school up the hill at the back of the house. I immersed myself in a new world of Simunul Bajaus, living in a house on the Sulu Sea. I learnt Simunul, ate dried fish and sambal, sat by the washing tap, went to weddings and made friends. I returned home for weekends but this constant coming and going took its toll on me and the children.

In August 1979, I left Sandakan. My field work was over. I had written a short history about Sandakan in its centenary year. But I had begun to fear for my sanity. I came to Kuala Lumpur, leaving my children behind. I had MR 400 from my freelance writing. It was my good fortune that Charan brought my children to me later in the year.

I applied for a job with the Sociology Department at the University of Malaya, but it did not happen. At the paper, when I asked the editor, Tan Sri Lee Siew Yee, for a job, he asked me to start immediately as a leader writer. I submitted the application a week after I started. It was a happy time at work, though the marriage was over. Early in 1980, Charan wound up his practice in Sandakan and came to Kuala Lumpur. It was too late. I had waited 13 years for him to come home. This time it was I who moved away.

Trying again

Two days after the decree absolute came through, I met Krish, my second husband. He was going through a painful separation and his wife had taken his son and daughter to India. Common friends told him I had managed to come through my divorce well. I gave in to the heady sensation of being desired. It was good to eat ice cream together on the beach, driving to nowhere just because we wanted to be together. I should have left it as a glorious affair. But I made the mistake of trying to make an honest woman of myself and convinced myself we should marry. My family felt they had not been able to help me when I was in trouble; now they didn't want to stand in my way when I was happy. But the turmoil continued, for Charan took the children away from this "unfit" mother and I had to go to court to get them back.

My mother and I talked about this, about what it costs children to go through divorce. But thinking back on our own experience, we knew that life for children in an unhappy marriage isn't good either. The trick was to have a happy marriage and neither of us had achieved that. But I was going to try again.

Mummy came to check out Krish in Kuala Lumpur and thought he was a "noble" man. Later, I discovered that she thought every man who liked me was "noble" and this characteristic vanished as soon as the relationship turned sour.

The children were older and they got a chance to be with my mother in their own setting. I don't know whether the visit left any impression on them but reminders of her Malaysian grandsons dotted my mother's place in Dharamshala. In the corridor opposite her bed was the bright orange and blue painting I had brought for Sunil on my visit to Indonesia. Mummy had liked it and Sunil had given it to her. For many years she treasured the baskets and bowls that Aman and Sunil had bought as goodbye gifts for her from the Chinese emporium near the house.

She ate papayas for breakfast and lunch, exulting in their sweetness. She discovered that soya bean curd was the Malaysian equivalent of *paneer*, Indian cottage cheese. It was a happy time. I had my mother, my children and the man I loved. I had a job I liked and I was soon invited by the Central Bank of Malaysia to write its history upon reaching its twenty-fifth year.

In February 1984, Krish and I went to Delhi to get married. In December 1985 he went to Melbourne to work and settle. I discussed the situation with my family in India. Again we took the risk assessment route. My relationship was already shaky, torn between him and my children. I could be looking forward to a life alone. It would be better for me to be in a country where it is easier to live as a single woman. Perhaps by going to Australia there could be hope for the relationship.

So I told Aman and Sunil I would be going to Australia and I would like them to come if that is what they wanted. Aman was 16, Sunil was 15. Aman wanted to stay with his father. Sunil asked for some time to think it over and then decided to come with me. Despite all my attempts to prevent them from having to choose between their father and mother, I had put them on the spot.

Sunil and I left for Melbourne in October 1986. The marriage ended eight years afterwards. I had been going to India every year but I don't think we talked much about my marriage. We talked about my life in Australia, the friends I was making, my work with a leading media group in Melbourne and my decision to go back to complete my PhD.

This time I decided to stay in Melbourne for myself and my son, rather than because of a man I was following. Good times came back again. The year I got divorced was also the year I finished my PhD. This was my present to myself. After completing a prize-winning PhD dissertation and my graduation, I came to Dharamshala in the winter of 1995 to visit my mother. Free again, and beginning a life of research and teaching.

Chapter 14

A soul mate

———

In Pashi's house in Amritsar, there are two photographs on the mantlepiece. On the right is one of her father, Professor Thakur Singh. On the left is one of her mother and mine, holding hands, looking young and beautiful and innocent. I had never seen a photograph of Pashi's mother. But more than that, it took me aback to see both of them together.

The relationship between Pashi's mother and mine became decidedly cool in the late 1940s. The immediate reason was that an engagement arranged between Ranjan and Pashi's eldest brother was broken from their side. But essentially it was the story of two women fighting over the same man. I ask Pashi in a veiled way, and she says, "No, no, they respected each other's spirituality."

Professor Thakur Singh was my mother's soul mate. There was a certainty about his love and friendship which my mother never had any reason to doubt. He was Bapuji's nephew, his brother's son, but more than that, he was Bapuji's devotee. From the early days in Rawalpindi, during Pitajee's illnesses, Bapuji trusted him to look after Mummy and he continued to do so for the rest of his life. There was a time when Mummy was travelling to Amritsar by train, and Professor Thakur Singh was there at the station as always to greet her. My mother saw that his leg had been injured. He had had an accident a few days before. "So why did you come?" she asked. He did not answer. She was arriving and so he came.

In him my mother had a friend and a soul mate that most of us yearn for, a person who was always supportive, always there for her. He was appreciative and encouraging. He was the one she would turn to for advice about her career or her studies. He helped her look after her finances, especially after she began to have trouble with her eyes. He was the one who accompanied her when she was taking up new appointments in Punjab, affording her the protection of family so that in this patriarchal society, she would not be perceived as a woman alone. He understood her grief and desolation at Bapuji's death, and her yearning for spiritual fulfilment.

Their lives were entwined in innumerable ways – through Bapuji, through Bapuji's family's love and regard for both of them, through Pitajee's love and affection for Professor Thakur Singh and Bapuji, through Pashi's love for my mother. Professor Thakur Singh had been part of our family since 1929 in Rawalpindi. Ranjan had stayed at their home in Ludhiana for a year when she was at school. It was Professor Thakur Singh who delivered my sisters back to our parents in Karachi when their school and college in Lahore closed because of the riots.

A broken engagement

There had been much coming and going between the two families. But early on, there must have been signs of disruption in the relationship between Mummy and Mrs Thakur Singh. Mrs Thakur Singh had no time for the *jatha* and its ritual dos and don'ts. She saw the *jatha* as the instrument for the closeness between my mother and her husband. Moreover, she could not have liked seeing Mummy's photographs all over their house.

Later in Delhi in 1949, a marriage was arranged between Ranjan and Professor Thakur Singh's eldest son, Inderjeet. Ranjan was 16 at the time and it triggered her enrollment for the BSc Home Science degree. Lata says that neither Pitajee nor Professor Thakur Singh's wife were keen on this match, seeing it as cementing a further bond between Mummy and Professor Thakur Singh. It was also interesting that the match had been arranged across caste lines. They were Jats, the dominant rural land-owning caste. We were Bhagars, an urban caste, not held in particularly high ritual esteem, but we had advanced educationally and professionally. But Inderjeet, Professor Thakur Singh's son, broke off the engagement, thus inviting his father's wrath. Father and son did not see each other for several years. The rift between my mother and Mrs Thakur Singh became permanent, though my mother downplayed it. Even when my mother was ill, living virtually across the fence in Khalsa College in 1970, Mrs Thakur Singh did not come to visit. Ranjan remembers that she was going over to borrow something from their house and my father asked her, "Did Mrs Thakur Singh come to call on you?" He told her not to go to their house.

Professor Thakur Singh continued to be part of our lives. He escorted me on my first trip to Punjab in the early 1960s, taking me to Jalianwalah Bagh in Amritsar, telling me how he was present when General Dyer shot at a peaceful assembly of 20,000 people on 13 April 1919. When I saw it, Jalianwalah Bagh was a dusty piece of ground. But this was sacred ground, for it was the site of a massacre that had fuelled anti-British sentiment throughout India. In 1919, Professor Thakur Singh had been studying at Khalsa College in Amritsar. The Principal had warned the students not to go to the meeting but, he said, "Nationalism was running hot in our blood." When Dyer and his soldiers started shooting soon after 4 p.m., Professor Thakur Singh found himself on the ground covered by dead bodies. Dyer and 50 soldiers shot at the people for 10 to 15 minutes, leaving at least 2000 people dead or wounded. The massacre was cold-blooded, with Dyer ordering his soldiers to shoot people running for the few exits. Professor Thakur Singh showed me the well where many had jumped to their death to escape the bullets. "There is the wall", he said, pointing to the south. "This is where many of us clambered up to escape, with the help of people from the nearby houses."

I went to Tarn Taran with him for the first time and plucked sweet corn from the fields. He took my children and me to the Golden Temple, on our Patti visit. Sunil remembered that visit 25 years later when he went to the Golden Temple with his wife, remembering that the marble floors used to be cold without the new matting that has since been put down. I still have one of the two steel *thalis* he gave me as *shagan* for the birth of my two boys. The other one is with Sunil. He bought them the photograph of the Golden Temple that is still on Sunil's dressing table.

He was a tall, handsome man. I did not see him in his heyday when he had been head of Physical Education at the Government College,

Ludhiana. I remember him always in a white *kurta* and pyjama with
a full grey beard, always smiling. It is difficult to think of him without
his bicycle. He rode it every day to the Golden Temple before dawn,
and was riding it into his 80s. My mother was also beautiful in the
photographs of that time.

Fruit in the evening

Their relationship was framed in familial terms. In one of the two
books on Bapuji and Bhai Randhir Singh they wrote together,
Mummy said of Professor Thakur Singh, "He is our first friend and
a sharer of our sorrows and joys." The more open the relationship
was, the more the questions remained unasked. For Pashi and her
family, my mother was Bhuaji (father's sister). After Professor Thakur
Singh retired, he stayed with Pashi. By then, Pashi was a widow with
grown-up daughters, and it was thought she needed the protection
of her father's presence. Pashi's mother went to stay with their older
daughter in Ludhiana, who was also on her own.

Every afternoon, Professor Thakur Singh would visit my mother,
always bringing bananas, for my mother loved fruit. He would then
take another lot of bananas home and urge everybody to eat. Pashi
loved her father and she loved my mother too. Visits were frequent
when Mummy was in Amritsar. Pashi continued to visit my mother
in Dharamshala after she moved there. She wrote to my mother
regularly, even after she went to live with her daughters in Sydney.
One of her letters arrived when I was visiting Dharamshala in
December 1995. By then, at my mother's urging, I had made contact
with Pashi in Sydney. It was Pashi whom I called from Melbourne to
come and be with me when Mummy died.

On our side in Delhi, we gradually stopped referring to Professor
Thakur Singh as Mamaji. When Mummy was in the Working Girls'
Hostel, Professor Thakur Singh used to come to Delhi to stay in
Bapuji's son's house. Mummy and I would visit him there, and I
noticed that she washed his clothes, which I thought was an inap-
propriate intimacy. He was the one person I knew who would take
precedence over me in my mother's affections. I was jealous of

his position in my mother's life. I remember visiting Mummy in Amritsar in the 1980s and seeing that his photograph was the largest one in her room, I put it away, bringing my family's photographs to the front.

My father was very fond of Professor Sahib. Once when Professor Sahib was visiting Delhi, he visited Pitajee in the clinic with Mummy and me. Pitajee's face lit up on seeing him and they talked of things I did not understand and people I did not know.

Lata says, "Pitajee was an unusual man. He was most broad-minded for people of that age. Aijee could never have had this relationship with any other husband." She says:

Pitajee knew that Aijee was very fond of Professor Thakur Singh. There was nothing hidden from him. The most remarkable thing was that he didn't resent it. When he was manic, he used to call him names but never when he was well.

Prof Thakur Singh

Mummy and Professor Thakur Singh's relationship was sustained for nearly 60 years till the end of Professor Sahib's life in 1989. Pashi recently told me how he had insisted on visiting Mummy in

Dharamshala the last summer of his life. He went alone, though he was over 90 and had had a cataract operation. The only concession he made in response to Pashi's concerns was that he took one bag of fruit for Mummy instead of two. It was on this visit that he fell ill. Mummy called Pashi and his son Amarjeet (Ami) and they all took him to Ludhiana. He died soon after.

Lata says:

When Professor Thakur Singh died, Pitajee wrote the most beautiful letter to his sons, Ami and Inderjeet. Aijee said that that letter was a great present to her. By Pitajee's letter being there, the relationship became joint. I believe the letter was so good that Ami read it to many people.

Chapter 15
Dharamshala, Amritsar, Delhi

My mother's last ten years were divided between Delhi, Amritsar and Dharamshala. Usually she stayed in Dharamshala between April and September. Between September and April, she stayed in a two-room unit opposite Banta Bhainji's place in Amritsar. She gave up the rooms when the landlady died. Banta Bhainji was having units built on the side of her house. The construction was rushed to enable Mummy to live there but, in the end, that is where her body was laid.

She visited Delhi in the winter mainly to see her brothers. Lata would come to Dharamshala to be with her, but Mummy knew that she had to go to Delhi to see her brothers. "I get famished otherwise", she explained when I asked why she continued to make the trip, even when she could hardly walk or see.

My mother's brothers, Swaran and Khojinder

The sense of her *paikai*, of her father's home as a sanctuary, remained important for my mother. At a particularly low point in

175

her life, she called Mama Khojinder's son Gurmit to come and take her home with him. It was Bauji's house, she said, the house of her father's son's son.

Mama Khojinder likes to remember his last conversation with her:

I said, "Bhainee [sister], stay a few days with us. You go to Gurmit's house and climb one set of stairs. There is only one more level of stairs." She said, "Khojinder, this time I promise. However I manage, I will climb the stairs, but this time I will live with you for quite some time."

His voice trembles. "She said, 'Khojinder when I see you, I remember Bauji. Your house is Bauji's house.'"

Mataji's daughter

After my mother's death, I go to Delhi for a few days in the winter to visit my uncles and sister and meet my old friends. Then I go to Amritsar and become part of a charmed circle of love because I am my mother's daughter. In India, Dharamshala has become my own place, where everybody calls me Mataji's daughter.

The unit looks much the same as it used to when my mother lived here. I have added my mother's graduation photograph and those of my sons and daughters-in-law to the picture gallery on the covered tin trunk. Swarna's room, later the store, is now my study. In the kitchen, I have added *murtabans,* the old-fashioned brown and white stone storage jars. I have installed a sink there too, thinking I would be washing my own dishes. Also a moon-cake lantern from Kuala Lumpur hangs by the kitchen. The one in the toilet has come apart.

For the last three years, Kanta has been coming for an hour-and-a-half every day to clean the house, do the washing and cut the vegetables. Until recently, the milkman used to come by in the morning. The paper man no longer delivers, and I have to go up to the market to get an English paper. The *dhobi* downstairs washes the sheets and towels and drycleans the shawls.

My morning routine is the same as before. I have my cereal

and tea, fill the water buckets and have my bath before going to the Gurdwara. I boil the milk and make sure I have enough boiled drinking water. Then, if the sun is out, I sit on the verandah and receive visits from my neighbours, get the latest news about who said what, who got drunk, who fought with whom, who has gone away to a wedding, and how the new couples are faring. They ask me about my sons and daughters-in-law. They want to see pictures of my grandsons. One year, I joined them in knitting in the morning sun. There are no questions about my work or even about the book I have been writing.

When the local sour lemon (*khatta*), is available, Bharjaiji makes the relish with sugar and fresh coriander and chillies. We sit on the verandah and eat it off pieces of newspaper.

My afternoon routine also remains unchanged. I read and then sleep for a while in the inside room. The children from next door drop in for a visit after school. Kaka (Gurwinder) from next door, comes to check out what is happening. He asks me for the prices of things and lets me know if I have paid too much. Did I buy brown bread for Rs 17 instead of Rs 14? Jaswinder now does not drop in for toast and jam as she used to do. She visits for a while but soon leaves. Arzoo, now in Plus One, comes in for conversation.

After that there are some more visitors, but not as many as before. Mummy's connections are now loosening, and mine are still shaky. My everyday contacts are now only with three households in the immediate neighbourhood – those of Bhaiji, Gurmeetji and Daljeet. With Tinku and his family there remains a closeness, and my closest companion there is Enu who is back home after doing her Masters degree in Kathak. The other children who used to come for English classes are now at university, doing courses ranging from agriculture to pharmacy. I try to visit other households when I am here, but find myself not wanting to impose unless they have given me a time. When I am alone again, I heat the milk to set the curd. Finally it is my time to write.

For the first five or six days I delight in the change of rhythm. I don't even go and check my e-mail at the neighbourhood Internet café, for I want life to go at a slower pace than it does in Delhi and Melbourne. I revel in the sparkling winter sun. Then the days get colder and the sun disappears. The snow-covered peaks are hidden by thick cloud. Gurmeetji asks whether she can hang her washing outside my window. There is nothing to see anyway. The neighbours do not come to sit in my part of the verandah. Everybody huddles in their own homes.

I have become tired of my own cooking. It is about then that I begin to plan trips of exploration in the Himachal or Punjab. One year I went to Chamba and Dalhousie and took the dangerous mountain road up to Bharmour. Another year I went to Patiala to visit the library at Punjabi University, famous for its collection on Punjab history. Twice there were weddings to attend in Amritsar. And more recently I got on a bus and went to Lahaul and Spiti.

I am not alone in the way that I am alone in Melbourne. Here the feeling of neighbourliness is strong and most often I delight in the constant coming and going. But after two weeks, I find myself going to check the e-mail to get back a sense of self, to reassure myself that I have another life in a university in Melbourne, even though few here are interested in it. They are just surprised that I am still "in service". Work begins to inch into my life in Dharamshala. I wonder what Mummy used to do at these times when small-town life begins to consume the rest of you. But perhaps in the summer and the monsoon months, the town is different. She had more visitors than I do. Bapuji would visit. ProfessorThakur Singh came every year. Pashi came. So did Banta Bhainji and her sister Sharan. Moreover, religion was the common bond between Mummy and her friends in Dharamshala.

I go to the Museum to check any recent additions and get enthused again about Himachal culture. I visit Sarika and Lochoe in their home on the hill on Khaneira Road, about three kilometres from Kotwali, and am plunged into the world of Tibetan art and food. I met Sarika, 29, in 1987 when she was learning how to paint Thangkas in Norbulingka, the Tibetan Cultural Centre about 20 minutes down the hill by bus from Kotwali. She is from Delhi and she is a sociologist. In Dharamshala that is enough of a bond. They are my friends here, in a Melbourne and Delhi kind of way. But as Sarika reminds me, I come and then I go.

The sun shines again and I look at the Dhauladhars, thick with snow. Just when I have once again built up an idyllic image of Dharamshala, the small town, I come down with a fever.

Fever

The fever is not high, but 101°F is respectable, even by my father's standards. I take some medicine and hope it will go away. I sleep the day away and feel sorry for myself. Jaswinder and Kaka come to check and I tell them I am not well. Daljeet from next door comes to visit.

I tell her I have fever, but am feeling better after the medicine. "Yes, I saw you sleeping all day", she says. "Didi, I have some rice and dal. Shall I bring them?" "No, no", I remonstrate. "I will have some milk and toast and go to sleep again." "I can make a *phulka* in no time", she says. I tell her I will just go to sleep.

"I have some Paracetemol", she says. I tell her I still have some tablets.

The next morning I feel better. There is no water in the taps, but some water is left in the tank. I manage to have a bath and go to the Gurdwara. "Have you been away?" some of the women ask. Back home, I sit in the sun, reading the paper. I am cross with Jaswinder and Kaka for they are making a noise next to me. "Go to your house", I say, "and jump there." I can hear myself sounding raspy.

Daljeet comes to dry the ingredients for *panjiri* on the wooden bed outside her house. Kaka goes to her and says, "Auntiji says, 'Go and play outside your own house.'" I feel mean.

I go inside to fry the onions that Kanta has cut. I sleep again for three hours in the front room. I think that this way I will be able to see the mountains. My remonstrance to the children has no long-term effect. Through a haze I can hear them outside the window. I can hear murmurs and then voices rising to a crescendo. I hear their father coming for his lunch. Every now and again I hear the sound of the stick used to scare away the monkeys. Is that water I hear? It is afternoon. It couldn't be. Somebody seems to be washing clothes somewhere. Through it all is the smell of fried onions.

Even under the quilt, I feel waves of cold. I again feel sorry for myself. Basically, I am alone here, just as in Melbourne. The small-town sociability is only a thin veneer, I tell myself. It is just me. I am not able to ask for help. Shall I call Sarika? I wish that Bharjaiji was here. With her and Arzoo, I have a generational relationship. But they have gone to Chamba. Tomorrow, when Ranjan Bhaini calls, I will tell her I have a fever. As soon as I am better, I will go back to Mamaji's house in Delhi.

I do not know that Gurmeetji has looked in through the window and found me asleep. I take my temperature. It is still 101°F. I take the last tablet. I garnish the dal, and eat some with the rice that Kanta has cooked and left for me. It is quite tasteless.

At 3.30 it is quiet outside. Daljeet's household has gone to sleep. I now find the silence overpowering. Slowly, I begin to feel better and go to the study. I do not know that Bhaiji has looked in. Seeing me busy at the computer, he had gone away silently.

Jaswinder comes in to say that today her father beat Kaka. "Kaka took off his clothes in the morning, and he did not want to have his bath and get his hair washed. Then Papa beat him so hard that it left a mark on his leg."

"Shall I show you the mark?" Kaka says. At that he rolls up his trousers and points to a mark I cannot see.

"Papa does not beat me", Jaswinder says. "I am scared of my father, so I always do what he wants. But Kaka doesn't."

Moving to another tangent, she says, "Today, Kaka does not want to have his hair up in a *jooda*. He wanted two plaits. Once when he had two plaits, the vegetable man, thought Kaka was a girl."

I tell them that among some American Indian tribes, the men wear their hair in plaits. That bit of information passes without comment.

"This afternoon", Jaswinder says, "the monkeys came. We were sitting and eating peanuts. A large monkey came. My mother scared him away with the stick. The monkey then went to your door and rattled it. Luckily you had bolted it from inside." She adds, "Once when I was having a corn cob, a monkey came and snatched it from my hand."

Kaka wants to have his say. "The monkey came to our house", he says loudly. "He pushed the door, opened the fridge, and took the bananas."

Seeing that I am suitably impressed, there is now silence. I tell them that I still have fever and am not very well. They leave.

Bablu comes soon after. I tell him I have fever. We have tea and I make him toast with butter. He doesn't want curd. I give Bablu some money to get me some more medicine. "Be sure to get it from the shop that Mummy used to get the medicines from", I remind him. He comes back in five minutes, saying, "Bhaiji has asked you to come down and have *phulkas* with *paneer.*"

I go down, ready to be looked after. Bhaiji's wife has come from Jammu to look after the household while Bharjaiji is away. Despite her protestation that she has not cooked for 24 years, she has cooked a tasty dish of *paneer*. Gurmeetji is also there. Devinder comes with a dish of *tandan*, the stalks of cauliflower. His wife, Maninder, has cooked it. They are good. I have two *phulkas* instead of one.

"What will you cook tomorrow?" I ask Bhaiji's wife. I feel connected again.

As I pass by Daljeet's house, I look in. There is the fragrant smell of *panjiri* cooking. She is roasting the *gram* flour in *ghee*. "Stay and eat", Daljeet says.

"Give Auntiji the *panjiri*," Kaka tells his mother, advocating on my behalf.

Panjiri is made every winter in Daljeet's house. "My mother-in-law used to make the *panjiri* and I learnt to make it there." Daljeet is the local expert on *panjiri*-making. When her brother's wife was expecting, she made 14 kilos of *panjiri*.

I ask about the beating this morning. She smiles for she is used to the children spilling the beans. The day before, it had been her beating Kaka as he threw somebody's drying coriander seeds in the dust. "What is to be done with Kaka?" Daljeet says. "He is so obstinate. He stood naked and would not have his bath. I was scared he would catch a cold. Then he jumped on his father as he was having his breakfast. His father gave him one. Kaka then came crying to me. I told him, 'See I told you to have a bath.' He did have his bath then."

Seeing Jaswinder and Kaka sitting with their father in the Gurdwara, faces uplifted to the hymns, there was little to discern of the drama that had gone before.

The *panjiri* is still being made. The *ghee* she is using comes from her mother-in-law in their village. They are going to Daljeet's husband's village later in the month. Daljeet says, "I always take or send *panjiri* to my mother-in-law."

I sleep, with the moon shining on me. I remember to be grateful that I live in two houses, in Melbourne and Dharamshala, where I can see the moon and stars when I go to sleep.

"Shall I tell you…"

There is no big drama, but the fever continues at 99.6°F. I don't go to the Gurdwara. Bhaiji comes to check on me, bringing me the morning newspaper. He is going to Kangra to have new glasses made.

Gurmeetji comes to visit with her grand-daughter. Jaswinder is ready for school but Kaka is jumping on the wooden platform near my chair, calling the vegetable man to come up. "Uncleji, Uncleji", Kaka shouts at the top of his voice. "Come upstairs." He repeats it a number of times.

Waiting for the vegetable man, Kaka and Kittu, a boy from down-stairs, play "vegetable man". Kaka places his hands on his head, and shouts, "Buy turnips. Turnips, turnips, turnips." Tiring of that, they play the body-kneading game. Kittu lies face down and Kaka gets on to his legs and begins pummelling them with his feet. My mother used to like me doing this to her. Finally the vegetable man comes with turnips, mustard leaves and a leaf new to me, cauliflower mustard. I buy a bunch for Rs 5.

Everybody in the neighbourhood is going to have spinach tonight. Gurmeetji sits outside her house cutting the mustard leaves with a scythe-like motion. Daljeet comes to sit by me and selects the good leaves and stems, placing them in a large aluminium basin. Maninder, Gurmeetji's daughter-in-law, sits in the sun, watching.

"You must eat with us tonight", says Daljeet. "I will make corn bread and mustard."

"You have to eat with us tomorrow", says Maninder.

Maninder, Daljeet and Bharjaijee have already started knitting jumpers for my grandson, Avjay. I am touched at this display of affection. In the afternoon, I sleep. The fever is not getting better. I think of going to a doctor but it is Monday and the market is closed.

Daljeet is standing outside and she comes to visit. I get up to make tea, but she remonstrates, "I will make it. You are a guest now for two days." I take a bowl of biscuits to her house. She makes the tea and places *panjiri* in the bowl I have taken.

I come back and Bindi, my cousin from Delhi, calls. We talk. There is little to do but show concern. He asks whether I am treating the fever. I feel that it is time to be with family again.

Next morning, I still have fever and go to the doctor. His clinic is a small, dark room with a pharmacy behind. In front of the table is a chair. There is a stool next to the doctor where the patient sits. And by the side of the room is a bench where other patients sit. It is a consulting and waiting room in one.

As it is early by market standards, the doctor is free to see me at once. He checks my throat, blood pressure and pulse, and asks what medication I have been taking. He says I have been remiss to have waited that long. I come away with two days worth of medicine that the doctor dispenses himself – antibiotics, analgesics and antihistamines. He tells me how and when to take the medicine, mentions that the tablets will make me drowsy and that I should take them after eating. Rs 40 for the medicine and consultation. "Come again in two days", he says as another patient arrives.

Kanta makes me two *phulkas* to go with the old potato curry that is already there. Kaka wants to eat some too, so he brings his own plate. As I am drifting off to sleep, Kaka sits companionably by me on the bed. Suddenly he says, "Give me a toffee, Auntiji."

"In the evening", I tell him.

Kanta goes away and I lock the door from inside and sleep. As soon as I open the door, Kaka comes in. He asks me, "Auntiji, do you have a stick?"

"No. No stick."

"We have a stick. Don't you have a stick?" he asks.

He comes and sits gently by me on the bed. "Shall I tell you about my uncle's village? In my father's village, there are two large houses. My uncle's house has biscuits."

"Shall I tell you, I saw a little dog in a box", he goes on.

"Are there dogs in your uncle's village?" I ask.

"No, but there is a big cat."

"Shall I tell you... shall I tell you..." he continues.

Later in the evening, as he sits with me in the study, he looks up at the wall, and there is a wooden walking stick hanging on the wall.

"Auntiji, you do have a stick", he berates me.

I had forgotten about it, I tell him. It used to be my mother's, before she got the ones from the United States.

He follows me from the study to the living room.

"Who is this?" he says, pointing to my mother's photograph.

"This is also your mother?" he points to another photo.

"Is this your grandfather?" he asks looking towards my father's photograph.

"Why are you wearing a hat?" he asks, looking at my doctoral graduation picture. "What are you carrying in your hand?" pointing to the rolled up degree.

Kaka goes out the door and comes back again bringing a bowl of *chidwa*.   "Do you have this?" he says.

I tell him that in Delhi we eat it fried, with spices.

"You eat it fried?" he repeats.

Some of the *chidwa* falls on the red carpet in the living room.

It is time for a toffee, for it is evening. "My toffee has a hole in it", he says, as he goes to put the wrapper in the wastepaper basket. He eats a bit of it, then the rest falls down. He goes to put the toffee in the kitchen garbage bin.

"Auntiji", he starts again. "Autiji, are these your children?" pointing to more photographs. "And these? And these?"

By this time, I am ready to lock the door again.

Remembering Mummy

The festivities begin a week before Guru Gobind Singh Ji's birthday in January. This year the children of the neighbourhood get up at 5 a.m. to assemble in the morning to say their prayers. Then the rest of the neighbourhood gathers in the misty wintry morning to walk through the streets of Dharamshala, holding up the Sikh flag, beating drums and cymbals while singing hymns. People join us at different points in the procession. It is back to the Gurdwara for prayers, tea and an early breakfast.

The hall is full on the actual day of the birthday. Hymns are sung all morning. The cooks are preparing the *langgar*, the ritual meal which will be served to thousands from the town after the prayers. As the morning prayers come to an end, there is a speech from the front by a member of the Gurdwara Committee. He notes the contribution of the children during this Gurpurab. He doesn't mention his own role in harnessing the children's enthusiasm. I am sitting towards the back of the congregation in the only space I can find. Then I hear my mother's name being mentioned, how Mata Inder Kaur started the children's Punjabi school and how that legacy has continued. He announces that in the building extension that is going up, they will name a room after her. My eyes fill with tears and I have a lump in my throat. Fourteen years after her death, my mother is still remembered with honour in Dharamshala.

Just as I am regaining my composure, I hear my name mentioned, how I have my home in the Gurdwara Building, and how I have been teaching English in the evenings. I am to go forward to receive the honour of the blessed yellow cloth draped around my neck. I recognise they are honouring my mother, but they are also acknowledging me as part of the community.

Leaving Dharamshala

The goodbyes start three days before I leave. Dinner at Daljeet's, dinner at Gurmeetji's, dinner at Bhaiji's place. Before that, tea at Baljeet's. On the final day, lunch at Tinku's place.

I now have my ticket and will be going around 6 p.m. I am going by the airconditioned bus and so I don't need to take the quilt on board. I have telephoned Delhi to say I am coming. Despite the airconditioning, it is going to be cold. I wear the skivvy, the usual woollen suit and a pullover. I cover my head with a shawl. I also have a parka, just in case. I also put the Himachal woollen socks over the ordinary ones.

Together with Kanta, I pack up the house. The carpet in the living room and the rug in the second room go into the box bed with naphthalene balls, as does the quilt I have been using. The curtains in the living room and the second room I leave hanging up. The photographs go back into the tin trunk in the living room. The books go into the tin trunk in the study. It is now full and difficult to close.

The *bagh* from the study is folded away. The small blue *durries* go into the front rooms. The kitchen takes longer to pack up. Kanta has washed the dishes. When they are dry I put most of the dishes away in the kitchen cupboard.

I still have the packing to do. Before that, I close the door, so that Kaka does not have a field day with his questions. I am finally packed. My laptop, a haversack with food and water and a bag with my clothes and papers. Most of the books I brought with me from Delhi I leave in Dharamshala. The others I have posted to Australia.

Gurmeetji makes me two potato *paranthas* for the journey. Kaka insists that his mother give me two oranges. Tea and *panjiri* at Daljeet's and then Bablu comes for my luggage. Bhaiji and his wife, Bharjaiji, Gurmeetji and Bablu come together for the goodbyes. Devinder drops by. Harpal, my neighbour opposite has offered to take me by car to the bus stop, for the airconditioned bus does not stop near the Gurdwara. I get in the car, put my hands together to say *Sat Sri Akal*. Five minutes later, I settle myself in a half-empty bus.

The Inder Kaur Scholarship

The Inder Kaur Scholarship was established in 2011 to honour Inder Kaur's initiative, daring and persistence in following her dream of education. If you are female and have financial difficulties, this scholarship can provide you with $7,000 per year for up to three years of your standard full-time program duration. To be eligible for this scholarship you must:

- be a female Australian citizen, an Australian permanent resident, a current or past refugee, or the daughter of a past refugee
- be full time enrolled at RMIT in a bachelor degree
- be able to demonstrate financial difficulties and/or educational disadvantage
- be passionate about education.

Preference will be given to commencing students with financial difficulties who are current or past refugees, or the daughter of a past refugee.

http://www.rmit.edu.au/scholarships/inder-kaur

Amino Hussein received the scholarship in 2012. She arrived in Australia as a refugee from Somalia. When she was awarded the scholarship, she was a full time third year student studying nursing. She was also working and had three children under the age of four.

Meena Amiry was awarded the scholarship in 2013. She is a refugee from Afghanistan and a first year student studying for the Bachelor of Arts (Criminology and Psychology).

Readings

Chapter 1 Dawn in Dharamshala

Bhai Sahib Randhir Singh Trust. 1993. *Autobigography of Bhai Sahib Randhir Singh,* 2nd edn. Ludhiana: Bhai Sahib Randhir Singh Trust.

Negi, A.S. 1994. *Dharamshala.* Hamirpur, H.P: The author.

Sharma, Neena. 1987. Women Leaders of Quit India Movement in the Punjab. Proceedings, Punjab History Conference, 21st session, March 27-29, pp. 421-424. Patiala: Department of Punjab Historical Studies, Punjabi University, Patiala.

Chapter 2 Nanaji

Bhatia, Shyamala. 1987. *Social Change and Politics in Punjab, 1898-1910.* New Delhi: Enkay Publishers Pvt Ltd.

Griffin, L. H. & Conran, W. L. 1940. *Chiefs and Families of Note in the Punjab,* vol. 2. Lahore.

Kaur, N. 1987. *Development of Postal System in the Punjab under the British.* Paper presented at the Punjab History Conference, March 27-29. Patiala.

Singh, Bhagat. 1983. The Ahluwalia Ruling House. *The Panjab Past and Present.* Jassa Singh Ahluwalia Number, ed. Ganda Singh, vol. XVII-II, serial no. 34, pp. 233-260.

Singh, Ganda. 1990. *Sardar Jassa Singh Ahluwalia* (S.S. Bal, Trans.), pp. 3-4. Patiala: Publication Bureau, Punjabi University, Patiala.

Chapter 3 The Girls Ate Last

Bhatia, Shyamala. 1987. *Social Change and Politics in Punjab, 1898-1910.* New Delhi: Enkay Publishers Pvt Ltd.

Chapter 4 Married in Rawalpindi

Bhatia, Shyamala. 1987. *Social Change and Politics in Punjab, 1898-1910.* New Delhi: Enkay Publishers Pvt Ltd.

Chapter 5 Chasing the Past

Douie, J.S. 1994 (1916). *The Panjab, North-West Frontier Province and Kashmir*. Delhi: Low Price Publications.

Bhatia, Shyamala. 1987. *Social Change and Politics in Punjab, 1898-1910*. New Delhi: Enkay Publishers.

Menon, Ritu and Bhasin, Kamla. 1998. *Borders and Boundaries: Women in India's Partition*. New Delhi: Kali for Women.

Superintendent of Government Printing. 1984 (1908). Imperial Gazetteer of India: Provincial Series Punjab, vol. II, The Lahore, Rawalpindi and Multan Divisions; and Native States. Delhi: Usha Publications.

Chapter 6 Ecstasy and Madness

Singh, Thakur. 1982. *Purab janam ke mile sanjogi: Jivani Sriman Bau Mal Singh Ji ate sambandhat prasang Bhai Sahib Randhir Singh Ji*. Amritsar: Shura Masak Pantar.

Sura Parwar, Amritsar. 1990. *Jivan Charitr: Bhai Sahib Bhai Randhir Singh Ji*, 4th edn. Amritsar: Sura Masak Pantr.

Chapter 7 Our Stories of Partition

Butalia, Urvashi. 1998. *The Other Side of Silence: Voices from the Partition of India*. New Delhi: Viking.

Singh, Ganda. 1997. A Diary of Partition Days. In *India Partitioned: The Other Face of Freedom*, vol. 11, ed. Mushirul Hasan, pp. 27-86. Delhi: Roli Books.

Chapter 11 The Working Girls' Hostel

Sharma, K. 1987. *Bhakti and the Bhakti Movement: A New Perspective*. New Delhi: Mushiram Manoharlal Publishers Pvt Ltd.

Chapter 14 A Soul Mate

Ram, Raja. 1969. *The Jallianwala Bagh Massacre: A Premeditated Plan*. Chandigarh: Punjab University Publication Bureau.

www.ingramcontent.com/pod-product-compliance
Lightning Source LLC
Chambersburg PA
CBHW052130270326
41930CB00012B/2825